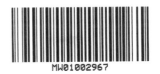

Think Like a Winner, Act Like You Won

Unleashing POWER, PURPOSE, and VICTORY in Your Life

By Carl Mathis

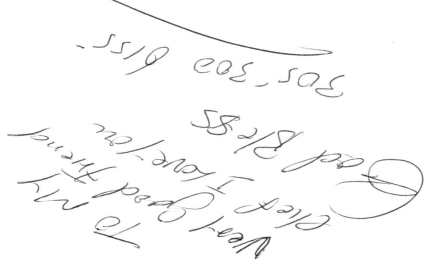

Acknowledgments

There are several wonderful people who motivated and encouraged me and contributed in countless ways to my experiences in writing this and other books.

My gratitude always goes to my mother, Melina Antoine Mathis, and the rest of my family. I thank you, Claudette and Haseland Mathis—you always encourage me to pursue my dreams. I will always appreciate the love and support you all gave me.

To my three sons: Jaron Mathis, Carl Mathis Jr., and Torrey Mathis. May the blessings of this life be all you could imagine.

I thank my spiritual leader, Pastor Angela Giles, and my church family at Holy Ghost Tabernacle of Deliverance Ministries in Miami, Florida, for their support.

Thanks to PR marketing team and editor, Marina Woods and company.

I dedicate this book to all who desire to move up the ladder in life and be successful.

CONTENTS

Introduction: Pre-Game Warm-Up 1

Chapter One: The Origin of Winning (On Your Mark, Get Ready) 2

Chapter 2: Think Like a Winner 15

Chapter 3: Choosing to Win 35

Chapter Four: Becoming a Winner 63

Chapter Five: Ignite Your Desire..94

Chapter 6: From Dreamer to Doer 104

Chapter 7: Your Attitude Determines Altitude....................123

Chapter Eight: Living Your Best Life 143

Chapter Nine: Winning the Battle for Your Mind 161

Chapter Ten: First Impressions Count (Shine, Baby, Shine)170

Chapter Eleven: You Are What You Think 180

Chapter Twelve: Act Like You Won 204

Chapter Thirteen: No Pain, No Gain.................................213

Introduction: Pre-Game Warm-Up

Think about this for a moment: you chose to open this book and read it. You could be doing so many other things right now, such as watching your favorite television show or your favorite sports team. However, you decided to seek after information that has a purpose and power and can give you the tools you need to be victorious in your pursuit. And you made an excellent choice! We live in an information-driven world. Information is power. However, information alone is like a dream stuck in the depths of your mind with no action to drive it home.

If you add action to what you learn from reading *Think Like A Winner, Act You Won*, here's what you'll get: SUCCESS. You can expect to be successful in whatever you do when you take a stand and actively move toward meeting your goals and fulfilling your dreams. That means you must do something! By picking up this book, you are unleashing power, purpose, and victory into your life. Whether you have the courage to finish this book and put your dreams into action is up to you, but if you are the winner I believe you are, I hope everything I've set out to share with you in this book helps you to make a wise decision!

Chapter One: The Origin of Winning (On Your Mark, Get Ready)

"The key is not the will to win … everybody has that. It is the will to prepare to win that is important."

~Bobby Knight

You cannot buy success.

Winning is not something you can acquire with money—no matter how much of it you may have. You cannot walk into a store or surf the Internet to purchase some magical product that leads to instant success, although there are plenty of marketers out there who will try to convince you otherwise. I'm sure you've been lured at one time or another by a commercial, billboard, or pop-up window promising you a simple and quick path toward success. You've likely seen ads like these:

> Want to lose weight fast? Take this diet pill and watch the pounds melt off!
>
> Begin earning up to $10,000 a day right away—while working in your pajamas!

Those aren't real advertisements, but they mimic what you've seen before. And they can lead to serious problems for the seller and buyer when they don't live up to the billing. There was a popular weight-loss supplement in the early 2000s that promised to "magically cure, alter, or fix our physical displeasure" safely and easily.[1] Who doesn't want to look like a digitally altered celebrity within no time? Sadly, that desire proved to be dangerous for many consumers of that supplement. It even led to death. As it turned out, the drug contained a substance banned by the FDA, and that substance caused many health problems for its consumers. The company ended up losing over $23 million in a lawsuit all because it promised something it really couldn't deliver—quick and easy weight loss in a safe manner; people looking for a shortcut to weight-loss success swallowed the promise only to end up worse than before.

The moral of that story (and so many like it) is there are no shortcuts across the finish line. Whether you're trying to get in shape, start a business, get out of debt, write a book, find lasting love—whatever you're seeking to achieve in your life—you must take the scenic route.

Winning is a process. You can only win by actively doing what's necessary to obtain the ultimate prize, which is success. And it's a good feeling when you cross that line toward victory. Some people believe in luck, chance, or the roll of the dice. Others believe in allowing nature to take its course and settling for wherever they end up. But if you want to be a winner in life, you can't dodge the process because it's the process that ultimately leads to success.

---

1 http://listverse.com/2016/06/02/10-false-advertising-promises-that-cost-companies-millions/

In most things you set out to accomplish, you will not achieve overnight success. You become a winner by doing what's necessary on a day-to-day basis to fulfill your goals. For example, let's say one of your goals is to start your own business. You must take all the necessary steps to launch the business, including deciding whether you're selling a product or providing a service, identifying your brand, developing a business plan, applying for a business license, setting up your office, and prospecting for clients. Then there are the ongoing tasks of running the business, including producing the work or delivering the service, managing the books, and pressing through rejection and setbacks (when prospective clients and customers say no to what you're selling). That's just an overview of some of the things involved in starting and running a business. It takes hard work and requires persistence. And the more you work at it, the more you train your mind to believe that winning is possible for you, no matter how overwhelming the task. That goes for any goal you set out to achieve. Diligently doing the work will produce results. What is diligence? It is a continuous effort. You are not born a winner; you become a winner by first deciding you indeed want to succeed and then by putting in the effort.

People who find it difficult to achieve success constantly look for loopholes, talk about their dreams but do nothing to fulfill them, or engage in time-wasting activities that have no purpose or meaning toward realizing their dreams. Although they're doing nothing that could drive them toward the winner's circle, they desire to become winners. That's not the way it works at all. If you plant an apple tree, certainly you don't expect to get grapes from that tree. So, don't expect to win if you are constantly doing things contrary to becoming a winner.

So, what gives? Why might a person who desires to win be doing everything to undermine that desire? The problem begins in the same place where the key to winning begins: your mind.

Can you fulfill your destiny without possessing a winning mentality? The answer pretty much is no. And it may be that you're not aware that your outlook is preventing you from succeeding. That outlook could be a lack of confidence in your abilities fueled by insecurity or low self-esteem. It could be a tendency to focus on what you lack regarding resources instead of focusing on what you do have to move forward (excuses). Or it could be a refusal to be open to all sorts of possibilities or the unwillingness to learn and grow (stubbornness). Motivational speaker Les Brown says, "There are winners, there are losers, and there are people who have not yet learned how to win." In this fast-paced, ever-evolving world, if you want to succeed, you must be willing to recognize and adapt to the times. Some people insist on doing things only in the way they are accustomed to doing them, but winners know they need to be flexible and are willing to adapt to a new way of doing things.

Some people make up in their minds that they are winners; these are the ones who will do whatever it takes to accomplish their goals. Then there are those who are content with their current situation; however, these same people constantly complain and are jealous of the person who decided to do something to become a winner in life. If that describes you, don't be a party pooper—get off your *butt* and do something productive that will get you closer to your goal. For example, do you only daydream about finishing that book you started writing decades ago? Decide that you're going to finish it. Develop a mental picture of yourself finishing. Then get up, dust off your draft, and begin writing again. And to make sure you keep writing, create a daily writing plan and follow it diligently. Take your eyes off what others are doing, and focus your energy on your dream and what you have in you to fulfill it. I promise that you will not be disappointed with the result.

I want to focus more on the mindset because one of the biggest challenges to living a fruitful life is trying to harmonize winning with the way we typically think. So how do we typically think? For starters, most people tend to react to what they see in the natural and internalize the event instead of isolating it. Let's take a situation in which a young woman is attracted to a young man but discovers he likes her friend instead. If she has a mindset weakened by insecurity and self-doubt, she'll wonder what's wrong with her and apply his rejection to how all men may see her; if it's fueled by jealousy, she may become upset with her friend for being chosen over her. Can you see where I'm going with this? Her negative response to that experience may impact how she interacts with the opposite sex going forward, particularly when it comes to issues of romance and courtship, and it may prevent her from being open to a healthy, positive relationship in the future because at the foundation of her thoughts and actions is her poor self-image. However, if she's confident in who she is as an individual and a woman, while she may be disappointed that the young man is not interested in her, she will recognize that his lack of interest has no bearing on her worth, and she can move on with her confidence intact.

How we think is often fueled by the way we see ourselves. In a recent devotion, Dr. Charles Stanley wrote that a negative self-image is a barrier to faith, in this case, our confidence to carry out our God-given assignments or achieve our goals. Other "faith barriers" to reaching the winner's circle in life include fear and doubt. Ultimately, "faith barriers hinder the flow of divine power in our life, slow spiritual growth, and prevent us from fully carrying out the Father's will."[2]

We are like magnets: we tend to draw whatever thoughts are in our mind. We will only produce like-minded things. Have you ever heard any of the following sayings before:

"If you want people to believe in you, believe in them."

"If you want people to trust in you, trust in them."

"If you want people to like you, try liking them."

How can you embrace winning without embracing a winning attitude? How can you become a winner without thinking like a winner? You can't because your thoughts and attitude dictate your actions, working together to dictate the outcome of your race toward success.

If you have yet to make up your mind that you want to be a winner (and I cannot imagine a soul who doesn't want to win), or you have not learned how to win, my objective is to show you how. So, my question to you is this: Do you want to be a winner, or do you want to remain in second place all your life? Nothing is wrong with being the runner-up if you tried your best. But let's face it: in most cases, no one remembers the person who landed in second place. The late Damon Runyon, a sports journalist for the *New York Times*, is credited with adding this twist to a familiar verse of Scripture: "The

---

[2] Stanley, Charles. *InTouch Daily Readings for Devoted Living*. July 2017. "Overcoming the Faith Barrier." (InTouch Ministries Inc.: Atlanta), p. 34.

race isn't always to the swift or the battle to the strong, but that's the way to bet."[3]

Make Up Your Mind

If you have been running in circles and not getting the results you want out of life, it's time to say, "Enough is enough" and make up your mind to change your outlook and begin doing something different, something that will get you closer to the winner's circle. Here's a story that illustrates what can happen if you don't make up your mind:

> A school-age boy complains to his parents about a bully that is taking advantage of him. Every day, the bully brazenly takes the boy's lunch and allowance money. But for some reason, the boy endures the abuse. He is hesitant to challenge the bully. One of his friends asks the boy why he allows the bully to harass him day in and day out, but he cannot give his friend a direct answer and walks away in silence. The taunting continues and escalates from the sling of words to the swing of fists. The bully adds injury to insult when he gives his victim a black eye and a swollen lip.

What will it take for you to say, "Enough is enough; I'm ready to be successful?" Would you allow a bad situation to

---

3 https://www.goodreads.com/quotes/123081-the-race-is-not-always-to-the-swift-nor-the

linger until it reaches a boiling point before you say it's time to make a change? Would you allow it to become unbearable before realizing that you need to put down your foot and take control?

So many of us wrestle quietly in frustration, hoping for our trouble or misery to disappear into the blowing wind. Some people wish and hope for something grand to happen to them without putting in the hard work it takes to prosper in life. That's why gambling in America is a multi-billion dollar industry. American gamblers lost—are you ready—nearly $120 billion in 2013.[4] Think about that for a moment. Those gamblers are probably like many people who look for a miracle to come out of nowhere and instantly make them rich. Wouldn't it be nice if something or someone could make you instantly successful with a simple yet magical touch? Imagine reclining lazily on your sofa surfing channels with a bowl of popcorn on your lap when a miracle worker shows up out of nowhere slightly tapping you on the shoulder. Then suddenly, wealth and prosperity are overflowing in your life. Wow! It's just a thought. Now let's return to the story about the boy and his bully.

Like that schoolboy who was being bullied, you are like a trash container, and—if you allow it— life's garbage will pour into you until it fills to the brim. Then the trash collector comes and empties the waste that's inside until it gets full again. Advertisements fill our minds with products or gimmicks that promise to make us thin, rich, or desirable without much effort. And social media, which monopolizes our time, tends to lull us into inaction and tempt us to live

---

4 http://theweek.com/articles/451623/how-did-americans-manage-lose-119-billion-gambling-last-year

vicariously through the highs and lows of those we follow instead of being about the business of establishing and fulfilling our own goals. No wonder we have such a difficult time developing a winning attitude.

If for any reason you cannot put the container by the curb so that the trash collector can empty it, garbage continues to be placed inside the container until it's running over. Likewise, the same negative and bad influences will keep pouring into your life. Life isn't always fair, even when you do everything right. However, if you keep filling your life with trash, it will eventually run over and become a stinking mess. And one thing about a problem, it's much easier to get into it than to get out of it.

The boy was hoping the bully would eventually stop on his own once he was satisfied that he had done enough damage to his young victim. Unfortunately, life won't stop hurting until you say enough is enough and decide to do something about it, something positive. You have the power to empty your container (your life) of the trash at any moment and move to the positive side of life.

In the boy's situation, power had been placed in the hands of the bully. The bully was controlling the situation. At any moment, he could decide to stop terrorizing the boy, as the boy's persistent silence signaled that he didn't want to be in charge of stopping his pain and struggles. If you keep silent, hoping that negative stuff in your life will eventually disappear, I'm here to let you know it will not. Just as the bully continued to taunt the boy, so will life continue to pummel you until you decide that you've had enough and you're ready to take over the reins. The truth of the matter is, life will keep on dumping on you if you continue to lie down and take it.

Remaining silent only enhances the fact that your life will not go the way you would like it to go. If you are not in control, someone else is, which means you can't direct the process of becoming a winner. People who don't do something about their lives will soon find themselves in a heap of trouble because they neglected to take a stand. No, you don't have to start a riot or use dynamite to blow up your life, but you need to know where to draw the line. If your life is not what it seems to be, if it's not working out for you, take control and say enough. Guess who had a moment like that in his life? A man named Barack Obama.

As a teenager growing up in Hawaii, the son of an American woman and an African man, Obama was suffering from an identity crisis. He neededed to belong but felt he fit in nowhere. As a result, he began to blow off his schoolwork and even experiment with drugs. His mother was afraid of the path he was on, but he eventually awoke from his temporary stupor and decided he didn't want to end up where he was headed:

> "Junkie. Pothead. That's where I'd been headed: the final, fatal role of the young would-be black man. Except the highs hadn't been about that, me trying to prove what a down brother I was. Not by then, anyway. I got high for just the opposite effect, something that could push questions of who I was out of my mind, something that could flatten out the landscape of my heart, blur the edges of my memory."[5]

---

[5] Obama, Barack. *Dreams from My Father: A Story of Race and Inheritance*. 1995, 2004. Three Rivers Press: New York, pp. 93-94.

Once Obama declared that enough was enough and decided to move toward more positive things in his life, like getting serious about school, it opened up all sorts of possibilities for him. And I don't have to tell you the level of success he ultimately gained as the result of his hard work and his refusal to give up even when he failed. He went on to become the first African American president of the Harvard Law review and the forty-fourth president of the United States, the first black man to hold that post.

Your life is too valuable to leave in the hands of bullies and negative thinkers. You cannot expect another person to take care of your needs; I discovered that several years ago when my wife died, and I ended up writing a book about it entitled *Life Is What You Make It*. You have the ability to say when you have had enough; your strength comes from taking control. Your future should be in your hands and not that of some bully's—whether it's a mean boss or a suffocating system—that's out to keep you from winning. You must take control of your life and stop being silent. Assume the reins and raise a standard as you shout, "Enough is enough! I want to be a winner!"

Win by Taking Action

I love watching professional sports. Football, basketball, and soccer are my favorites. What I noticed after a while is that when the season comes to an end with the championship game, almost immediately after that final match, it's as if there was only one team playing in the game. It's not supposed to be like that. After all, the other team made a valiant effort to win the championship, and coming in second place is not bad, right? But life is such that we all want to be the winner at the end of the day—and history seems to celebrate and remember only the winner.

Maybe you heard something different, but winning is not just for a select group of people—*anyone can win.* It doesn't matter whether your zip code is in the South or the North. It doesn't matter if you currently reside in a palace or live in subsidized housing. Winning is no respecter of persons. There is no favoritism or partiality when it comes to achieving success in one's life—*anyone can win.* The only person who can keep you from winning is the person in the mirror. You must decide if you want to win or not and then take action. So, go ahead and look in the mirror. Do you see that person looking back at you? Does he or she look familiar? Is that person a winner? Are you?

If you are always coming in second place, if you're always getting passed over for that promotion, if you believe you are the black sheep of the family, and you want to be recognized for your gifts, your contributions, and your accomplishments after it's all said and done, *Think Like a Winner, Act Like You Won* will show you how to leap over that second place hurdle and into first place.

This book is for people who want something better than what they have right now. It is for people who want to grow, who want to get beyond just dreaming and get to the business of doing. It's for people who are ready to ditch the excuses and courageously pursue every opportunity to go to the next level. It's for people who are sick and tired of being sick and tired, for people who are ready to walk the talk. Finally, *Think Like a Winner, Act Like You Won* is for people who are ready to win and won't stop striving toward their goal—even when they experience setbacks or failure—until they have reached the winner's circle. It will show you how to strive to be the best at whatever you do. Are you ready?

Okay, let's begin. Get on your mark, get ready, set … let's go!

Chapter 2: Think Like a Winner

"Imagination has a great deal to do with winning."

~ Mike Krzyzewski

Nick Vujicic is a man of many talents and hobbies. He's an author and actor who loves to paint, swim, and fish. He also skateboards, surfs, and golfs. He's a husband, father, and minister of the gospel. He stands three feet, three inches tall, and he was born without any limbs. That's right—he has no arms or legs. But that has not stopped Vujicic from fulfilling his purpose and living life to its fullest. And that's because he didn't allow his physical limitations to dictate his outcomes. He says, "Your circumstance doesn't have to determine your future, your happiness, and limit your joy."[6]

Despite being born with a severe physical handicap, Vujicic doesn't see himself as restricted in any way. Once he made up his mind that he could accomplish anything he set his mind to—with the help of God—he blossomed. Today he inspires millions of people around the world, not only with the good news but also with his life. If he can do all that without limbs, imagine what you can do with your limbs. As he demonstrates by his successful life, the power to do and be your best doesn't lie within your arms and legs or what you look like physically. It begins in your mind and rests in your heart. Can you see yourself winning?

---

[6] https://www.attitudeisaltitude.com/speaker/nick-vujicic/

The way you think can be the origin of your triumph or your agony of defeat. We often hear people say had they known "THIS" early in life, their life would have taken a different turn. The "THIS" they are referring to is that thing that could have catapulted their life toward success, but for whatever reason, they did not learn it. Take for example a middle-aged couple that didn't learn the importance of saving money and avoiding debt when they were younger. Over time, they spent more than they earned and often had to use credit cards when emergencies arose because they didn't have a reserve fund or enough savings. Before long, the couple accumulated nearly $100,000 in credit-card debt. They were drowning financially, and it was putting a strain on their relationship and eventually keeping them from fully enjoying their lives. Had they known when they were young what they came to discover as middle-aged adults, they would be in a different place today. But guess what, there is still hope for that couple.

Yes, they could be further along financially had they known to make wise money choices earlier in their marriage, but Debt-Proof Living founder Mary Hunt is the perfect example that it's not too late for them to turn it around and not only get out of debt but also prosper. You see, Hunt and her husband were once in that couple's shoes all because she spent money mindlessly and had no idea where it was going. But once she hit rock bottom, she decided to change her mind about the way she viewed and spent money. It took time, but Hunt made her way toward the winner's circle. Today she is a best-selling author who helps other families and individuals get out of debt and manage their money. Most of all, she has accumulated wealth, ultimately turning her situation around.

Obviously, I don't know what your "THIS" is, but whatever it is, you still have time to learn and master it, just as Hunt did. It's all in your thinking and doing.

The time you spend working on the way you think will determine whether you will win or lose. Many of us were taught from a young age by our parents or guardians to do things a certain way. And throughout our lives, we have adapted whatever we learned—and we master it. Some people learned sound principles that have benefited them in life. For example, if a parent teaches her son always to say thank you and consider others first, it's likely her son will grow up to be a chivalrous man who always opens doors for women or is pleasant to practically everyone he encounters. On the other hand, some people were taught some not-so-good principles as children—and often by example—that have only hurt them in life. Some parents treat their teenage or young adult children as if their children are their peers. The danger in that is that those children often have problems respecting authority figures because they see them as their equal, which can lead to unfortunate experiences in the workplace.

King Solomon put it this way, "Train up a child in the way he should go, and when he is old he will not depart from it" (Proverbs 22:6). According to the promise in this Proverb, a child or person who is diligently trained in the "way he should go" will remain faithful to that way in his life. Any individual who has been trained properly in the principles of life and has lived in harmony with them until he is old will not stop doing what has become second nature to him. Rarely do people abandon a positive way of living in their adulthood if it's the way they were taught to live when they were children.

What would happen if you applied that same principle to your thinking? What if you train your mind to think about the values of purpose, power, and victory? Even if you stray for a while, according to the principle of Proverbs 22:6, you will not abandon what you have learned. You will be successful in life if you train your mind accordingly. Even the Bible highlights the importance of renewing your mind (Romans 12:2). That means to come into agreement with your newfound life, as you may not be accustomed to thinking like a winner.

However, if you want to change your outcomes, you must change your thinking. You must be careful about what you meditate on because your thoughts will shape your life. Jesus said to a Roman officer seeking help for his ailing servant, "Go back home. Because you believed, it has happened."[7] Those words also apply to you and me.

Drawing from faith, patience, and belief, allow that little voice within to give you answers to the questions below. What do you have to lose by answering them? You have done it your way until now, so how about trying this way. Now begin writing.

What do you really want for yourself?

___

___

___

___

What do you really need in your life?

---

[7] Matthew 8:13, NLT

What will make you truly happy?

If you think like a winner, you'll live like a winner. Author Napoleon Hill put it this way, "Whatever the mind can conceive and believe, it can achieve." [8] "The mind is everything. What you think, you become. What you feel you attract. What you imagine, you create."[9]

Has anyone ever told you that you have more inside you than meets the eye? That means that there are more things inside you than you can see. Many people don't realize there are invisible abilities and visible abilities, internal power and external power. The greater of the two kinds of abilities are those that are invisible. Everyone knows that Michael Jordan is considered the best basketball player of all time—the G.O.A.T. in his sport. But did you know that Michael Jordan didn't make the varsity team at Emsley A. Laney High School in 1978? He was so embarrassed that he went home, locked

8 https://www.goodreads.com/quotes/77253-whatever-the-mind-can-conceive-and-believe-it-can-achieve

9 A quote often attributed to Buddha, but its author is unknown

himself in his room, and cried.[10] But that didn't stop him from trying. He eventually made the team; went on to play in college, where he helped lead his team to an NCAA championship; and he was drafted third in the 1984 NBA draft. The rest is history. He would go on to win six NBA championships for the Chicago Bulls, being named the Most Valuable Player in each championship run.

There was more in Jordan than even his high school coach could see back in 1978, but Jordan never let his defeats stop him from pursuing his goal. He credits them for his success—and that's because Jordan always believed in himself no matter what. He said, "I've missed more than 9000 shots in my career. I've lost almost 300 games. Twenty-six times, I've been trusted to take the game-winning shot and missed. I've failed over and repeatedly in my life. And that is why I succeed."[11]

Have you ever pushed yourself until you couldn't go any further? Have you ever gone so far away from what you were accustomed to, that you started wondering if you'd ever be that person again? If you have, then you know how overwhelming it can be to move out of your comfort zone. But the benefit of making yourself uncomfortable or pushing yourself that little bit further can be the breaking point for achieving your goals and reaching ultimate success. It's when you challenge yourself to push beyond what you're accustomed to that you will know what you're made of. Remember, no one ever achieved greatness while staying in his or her comfort zone. Motivational speaker Brian Tracy says you must "move out of your comfort zone. You can only

---

[10] http://www.newsweek.com/missing-cut-382954

[11] http://ftw.usatoday.com/2016/02/best-sports-quotes-about-winning

grow if you are willing to feel awkward and uncomfortable when you try something new."[12]

First, you must know what *your* comfort zone looks like. In general, a comfort zone is a place or situation where one feels safe or at ease and without stress. Think of a baby living inside its mother's womb. The estimated period is nine months. During that time, the child is most comfortable (I cannot speak for the mother!). But there comes a time when the baby's growth will supersede the space inside the mother's womb. The baby can only grow to a certain size and weight before it has no choice but to come out—one way or the other. In some cases, the mother must be cut by a doctor who must pull the baby out. Just like a baby, you must come out of your little bubble to grow and experience new and exciting things.

Please don't misunderstand what I'm saying. There's nothing wrong with being in your comfort zone, but once you get too comfortable and start holding back out of fear instead of challenging yourself to learn, grow, and try new things, you have a serious problem. I love the way Thomas Edison puts it, "We shall have no better conditions in the future if we are satisfied with all those which we have at present."[13]

Many have fallen short in life when it comes to developing those hidden things inside them because they never broke the shell of comfort around them. Many things are buried inside you that need to be developed. For one, your character. How you act (what people see) is the result of your character (what's inside you). Your character is developed by your thoughts. How you think will determine how you act. So,

---

[12] https://www.brainyquote.com/quotes/quotes/b/briantracy391332.html

[13] http://www.notable-quotes.com/e/edison_thomas.html

whether you win or lose, it all begins with how you think. Your thoughts are the genesis of everything.

The mental state of your mind is powerful. It has been said that an average human only uses 10 percent of his brain daily. Can you imagine what would happen if you could tap into the other 90 percent? Whether you believe that to be true or not, we could do more to develop our inner strength since the mind is the birthplace of who we are and who we become. If we dedicate more time and effort to developing our brains to get the results we want, success will be imminent.

In this age of technology, when people talk about success, they often mention networking and personal development, which are important. However, often missing from the conversation is the subject of your mindset. A positive and fully developed mindset is what separates the winners from the non-winners. You can achieve great success in every area of your life if you've set your mind on thinking like a winner.

Character Is Critical to Your Success

Your character comprises the mental and moral qualities distinctive to your unique personality. And winners are known by the mental and moral qualities they exhibit every day in any given situation.

What is moral character, and do we need it to live a healthy and prosperous life? Moral character can be defined as a set of qualities that makes somebody distinctive, especially as it relates to her state of mind and how she expresses her feelings. What comes to mind are qualities such as integrity, courage, and a conscience of what's right and wrong. It's innate qualities like these that attract others. So, when you set out to accomplish a goal, your moral compass is almost as critical in guiding you toward success as your outlook. Your moral character also shapes your thinking and informs your attitude. It is your public reputation—shaped by how honest of a person others view you to be—that is on display for others to see, and they will judge you by it. The right attitude will draw the right people to you. So, let's examine what it means to be poor in spirit.

To be poor in spirit is to realize that nothing you have is more important than achieving your specific goal. Knowing this, you should be willing to part with anything that may hinder you from achieving your goal. That is why Jesus said, "*No one of you can be my disciple who does not give up all his own possessions*" (Luke 14:33). When you show that you are willing to give up whatever it takes to be successful, it will produce great results. It has been said that your attitude determines your altitude. How you think and feel about yourself and your ability to succeed at whatever you set your mind to will determine how far you'll go or high you'll climb the ladder of success.

Attitudes are the established ways of responding to people and situations. Your beliefs or values typically shape your attitude, which is manifested through your behavior. If you take your attitude and apply it toward achieving your goals, nothing will be able to prevent you from reaching your destination. Anything that stops your progress will be deemed a hindrance. Relationships, possessions, and even ideas can all be hindrances if they block your productivity. The most important thing is what you are willing to give up to accomplish your goal. So, you must decide if the thing that prevents you from obtaining what you're seeking is worth giving up. Is it a relationship that's stifling your growth? Is a dead-end job that you've long outgrown? Is it a bad case of self-doubt? Is it a non-supportive friend? If you find that you're having trouble achieving a goal, what is standing in your way? When you identify the answer, you must make an important, life-changing decision of what is more important to you: your goals or the thing that hinders you.

Attitudes will drive your behavior! Even your body language is a result of your mental attitude. Whatever you think and meditate on will eventually show up in your posture, your facial expression, your walk, and so on. When choosing your attitude, you emit that mood and send out a message that everyone around you pretty much understands, consciously or unconsciously. In other words, your attitude is your first line of exposure to a person.

You should live by a code of ethics and a standard of conduct, especially if you want to live a healthy and prosperous life. You must keep in mind that attitudes shaped by moral character contrast positive values with negative values. To achieve success, you must express a positive attitude overall and not in isolation.

A few thoughts concerning your attitude going forward

- Consider acting respectfully at all times. Doing so will allow you to achieve success faster and more efficiently.
- Make it a priority to be honest with all people drawing on your inner strength.

- The abuse of your power and privilege has no place in your attitude. Use your ability to inspire to motivate yourself and others.
- Avoid causing harm to anyone. Instead, actively seek to treat others well. When you respect others, you will encounter fewer difficulties on your path to success.

It's not what happens to you that matters but how you react to what happens to you, especially when unexpected challenges arise. What you must do is develop and master strategies that will help you think and act positively and creatively on a consistent basis.

When someone talks about you, what would he or she say? When that person places you in a category, where would he or she place you? What that person says and where he or she places you determines how others see you and can affect how far you go. For example, being successful is associated with a character. No one would give you a chance in hell if your character is shady and hints at trouble. Your character will speak volumes about you and your potential, and a sound character will pave the way to success.

Bringing out your character starts with the choice you make to go for your dream. Keep in mind when you make that decision, it will cause uncertainty. However, no matter how skittish you feel, you must remain committed to your decision. Let's face it: if you aren't at least a little concerned, your dreams are probably not big enough. Your dream should be so big that even if you fall a little short of reaching the pinnacle of it, what you do achieve is still mind-blowing. Dreaming big and going for it requires change and a little uncertainty.

The risk comes from change. When we move out of our comfort zones, it creates suspicion because we're moving into unfamiliar territory. But don't worry. It's all a part of the process; you're changing for the better. I know it's not easy to modify the way you've been doing something almost all your life. Adjusting the way you think about yourself or specific situations can be difficult, but it's something you must work at diligently until your new and improved outlook becomes your automatic thought pattern about any given matter. Look at it this way: what you have been doing all your life got you to where you are right now, a place where you don't want to be (or stay). So, couldn't a new way of thinking take you where you need to be? Now, don't you think it's a good idea to change?

Character Develops Thinking

Your mindset determines whether you win or lose. In other words, your success is determined by how you think. If you have a negative thought, you must counteract it with a positive one. I realize that is easier said than done. I know from personal experience. But just as I realized that changing my thoughts was a great challenge, I also knew that it was the key to creating a new mindset and opening doors to opportunities I never thought possible before. Most of the time, we're fearful of what's to come, but if we are determined to become winners in life, we must force ourselves to keep moving forward and always to think positively. Trust me: your new thinking will never acclimate to your old ways of doing things.

In the greatest book of all time—the Holy Bible—Jesus puts it this way, "No one puts new wine into old wineskin, for the old skins would burst from the pressure, spilling the wine and ruining the skins. New wine is stored in new wineskins so that both are preserved."[14] What does that mean? The simplest way I can explain that Scripture is that new ways of doing things are not compatible with the old ways. As a result, the mind needs to transform so that it can be conducive to the new ways. If you process new information with an old mindset, you won't be able to understand the information. Trying to do so would be a waste of time and energy. Is processing new information with a new mindset easy to do? Of course not!

Compliance is the greatest threat to moving into something different. Most if not all humans are creatures of habit. We are comfortable with doing things a certain way and find it difficult to change. But to think like a winner, you must be willing to detach from your old ways of doing things to form new habits and find new opportunities. Don't allow yourself to be boxed in by a one-track mindset. A whole world of untouched possibilities is waiting for you. But it's going to take your changing from the old to the new to discover it.

Your Actions Project Your Character

Your character is the total of all the qualities that make you who you are: your values, your thoughts, your words, and your actions. First, let's talk about your values.

Values are the things you believe are important concerning the way you live and work. They should determine your priorities and, deep down, they're probably the measures you use to figure out whether your life is turning out the way you

[14] Matthew 9:17

want it to. So, you must decide what's important to you. What is the one thing that will make you want to do whatever it takes to become a winner? If it's valuable to you, it should give you the desire to push beyond the obstacles that impede you from achieving it.

> "Be fearless. Have the courage to take risks. Go where there are no guarantees. Get out of your comfort zone even if it means being uncomfortable. The road less traveled is sometimes fraught with barricades, bumps, and uncharted terrain. But it is on that road where your character is truly tested. Have the courage to accept that you're not perfect, nothing is and no one is, and that's okay." -Katie Couric[15]

Now, let's talk a bit about the connection between your character and your behavior.

The Greek defined character as a "branding mark" on products, or an engraved or stamped mark on coins or seals. It's a word that may refer to any artificial symbol or sign, and it often refers to human moral character involving assessments of mental qualities and moral virtues or lack of them.

How you act is "your brand." If you examine a commercial or any advertisement closely, you will notice that it has a unique label, look, or mark. You'll know whether it's pushing Pepsi or Coca-Cola just by the advertisement. You can recognize a pair of Air Jordan gym shoes just by the logo. If someone labeled you, would it be as a winner? Would it be

---

[15] https://www.values.com/inspirational-quotes/6763-be-fearless-have-the-coura-

negative or positive? Would it capture the attention of another person? These are some of the questions you need to ponder when developing your character, and if you don't like your answers, adjust your thinking and actions accordingly.

Maybe you realize this, and maybe you don't, but the people in your life contribute to the shaping of your character. People are critical by nature. We tend to judge others by what we see. If you keep surrounding yourself with people who are not interested in doing something positive with their lives, that's how others will judge you. I'm sure you've heard the adage "If you want to soar like an eagle, you can't hang with turkeys." If you're hanging with "turkeys," right or wrong, you will be characterized as someone who is not doing anything with his or her life. So distance yourself from those types of people. That doesn't mean you cannot love them from afar. (Some of those people may be your cousins!) But if you want to soar, you must remove them from your inner circle. The road to success can be a lonely one because not everyone around you is willing to do what it takes to get to the proverbial pot of gold just because you are.

You Are Your Thoughts

Thoughts are ideas, plans, opinions, pictures, and so on that are formed in your mind. When it comes to having a winning mindset, pay attention to what comprises your before you put them into action. Remember that your actions will define your character.

Think positive thoughts as often as possible, if not at all times. When your thoughts become action, that action should take you closer to your destination: WINNING. "Watch your thoughts; for they become words. Watch your words; for they become actions. Watch your actions; for they become habits. Watch your habits; for they become your character. Watch your character for it will become your destiny."[16]

Your thoughts will eventually become your future, so it's a good thing to develop and maintain a positive thought pattern. You may be familiar with Proverbs 4:23, which stresses the importance of guarding our hearts, where we pretty much house everything—our desires, our hopes, our dreams. I particularly like the New Century Version of that verse, which states, "Be careful what you think, because your thoughts run your life." So, what do you think about?

You Are the Words You Speak

Author and speaker Yehuda Berg wrote, "Words are singularly the most powerful force available to humanity. We can choose to use this power constructively with words of encouragement, or destructively with words of despair. Words have energy and power with the ability to help, to heal, to hinder, to hurt, to harm, to humiliate and to humble."[17] We can either use words to transform the way we think or use them to dig a deeper hole to the point of no return. "The words you say will either acquit you or condemn you."[18] What you speak can break you or make you, so always speak positive and

---

16 https://www.values.com/inspirational-quotes/3869-watch-your-thoughts-for-they-become

17 http://www.huffingtonpost.com/yehuda-berg/the-power-of-words_1_b_716183.html

18 Mark 12:37, New Living Translation

constructive words because it will benefit you tremendously in your walk toward success.

Your words don't just comprise sound emitting from your voice box. You can't just say anything because you feel like it. Your words have power—the power to change the course of your life for good or evil, the power to command success into your life. When you speak, speak as though you're standing atop the tallest mountain and raising your hands in victory. Speak like you know you have the power inside you.

God Himself created the world by the power of His words. Since we were created in His image and likeness, we acquired that same power given to us through our words. Words do more than convey information. The power of your words can destroy one's spirit, even stir up hatred and violence. Likewise, your words have the power to speak success and prosperity, and they also have the potential to cause severe damage.

As you begin to become more intentional about the words you use to describe yourself, your capabilities, and your future, start meditating on these truths:

- You are successful, and don't let anybody tell you differently.
- Where you live does not exemplify who you are or what you can become.
- The clothes you wear or the vehicle you drive cannot determine the person you are.

Remember, clothes don't make a person, but the person makes the clothes. The same goes for the vehicle you drive. The way you think will get you to the hilltop. Don't say you cannot purchase your dream home or travel the world. Don't say your credit is not sufficient to own houses and land—and please don't say you *can't*. The word "can't" should not be in your vocabulary. If it is, replace it with these words: "With men this is impossible, but with God all things are possible."[19]

If you desire to be successful, you must think positively and envision yourself winning. In May 2011, at age twenty-one, Derrick Rose became the youngest player in NBA history to win the Most Valuable Player award. The award is given during the playoffs, toward the end of the basketball season. But it was at the beginning of the 2010-2011 basketball season when Rose posed this question to journalists when asked about his expectations for himself that year: "Why can't I be the best player in the league? I don't see why [not]. Why can't I do that? I think I work hard. I think I dedicate myself to the game and sacrifice a lot of things at a young age, and I know if I continue to do good, what I can get out of it."[20] Rose saw the possibility in his mind. He believed without a doubt that he could be the best, and he worked his butt off to prove it.

You've likely heard this well-known quote, "Winners never quit and quitters never win."[21] By now you should have gotten the picture: if you want to progress in life, it's up to you. You can read plenty of books on how to become a go-getter and how to be successful, but if you don't apply action to your good intentions, all the knowledge from the books and speeches you ingest will be wasted. If you pursue your dream and don't give up, with God on your side, the sky is the limit.

---

[19] Matthew 19:26

[20] http://www.espn.com/chicago/nba/columns/story?columnist=isaacson_melissa&id=6463074

[21] www.brainyquote.com/v/vincelomba122285.html

God has given us the ability to communicate through the spoken word. It is a unique and powerful gift. Remember, our words can destroy or build up. With our words, we can command blessings in our lives and build ourselves up to be our best selves and make the sky the limit.

You are Action

Every living thing in life develops through progress. In other words, we all grow. Take a tree, for instance. It starts from a tiny seed and eventually grows to such a magnitude that we can climb it. But here is the kicker: growth for a living thing is not possible without being fed. Plants need water, fertilizer, nurturing, and so on to grow. In the same way, the human mind needs information to grow. And growth occurs when we take action, consistent and repeated action. We are not striving to be one-hit wonders!

Winners are not made overnight. Becoming a champion is not an instant accomplishment. It takes hard work and time, but with determination and consistency you can be a winner. It has been said that it takes approximately twenty-one days to create a new habit. Try this:

In the space below, share a current negative thought or action that you're willing to change for the better. Then practice thinking that new, more positive thought or acting out that new, more positive routine. Then pay close attention to what happens on day twenty-two and beyond.

____

____

This question has been debated and discussed many times: How does a person develop a winning attitude? No one is born a winner; with effort, you develop a habit or create a culture of success over time. One thing we know for sure is that everyone comes into this world butt naked, with a clean slate, and a basic desire to learn. Every single idea, desire, or belief we own today we were not born with; we had to learn and develop it. We had to learn how to walk, talk, read, and write—all done by creating a new habit.

How about we create a habit of winning.

Chapter 3: Choosing to Win

"You have to choose your path. You have to decide what you want to do. You are the only person that can determine your destiny."

~Lailah Gifty Akita

Actor Sylvester Stallone has been a household name since the mid-1970s. Today, the Hollywood veteran can command up to $20 million per film.[22] You've likely seen him in movies like *Rambo* and *Demolition Man*, but chances are you identify him most with the film *Rocky* and its many sequels. *Rocky* was so successful that many fans still see Stallone as the title character to this day. That could be because they commiserate with the hero who fights against all the odds to become a champion, to achieve the American dream. Rocky never gave up on his dream. And neither did Stallone.

The thing you may not know about Stallone is that he not only starred in the movie, but he also wrote it. Stallone is a good actor, but one reason he could play the main character so well is he knew what it was like to overcome a difficult obstacle standing in the way of one's dream. Here's what

[22] http://succeedfeed.com/the-inspiring-sylvester-stallone-success-story/

blogger and Successfeed.com founder Riz Pasha writes about Stallone[23]:

> Sylvester Stallone's story is one of rejection, struggle, persistence, overcoming odds and definiteness of purpose and there is something we all can learn from the man. Stallone had crystal clarity on what he wanted. He wanted to be an actor, but it wasn't going to come easy for him. His first obstacle standing in front of him was the fact that the lower left part of his jaw was paralysed, which not only gave him a unique expression but also slurred speech. Agents laughed at him, and he was rejected over 1000 times because of his disability. Let me repeat that—rejected over 1000 times.
>
> But that didn't stop a broke and struggling Sylvester Stallone. He was determined to achieve his goal.
>
> To keep paying the bills, he even went as far as stealing his wife's jewelry and selling it. Not long after he found himself homeless and sleeping at the New Jersey bus terminal for three weeks. Things got so bad for him that he had to sell his best friend, his dog, to some random guy at a liquor store for a measly $25 because he couldn't afford to feed him. Stallone loved his dog and walked away from the sale crying.
>
> Upon watching a fight between Muhammad Ali and Chuck Wepner, Stallone got an idea for a movie script and immediately took action. He didn't sleep the entire weekend and wrote for twenty hours straight until it was complete.

---

[23] ibid

His plan was to play the lead in the movie so that he could get his big break into acting but again he faced massive rejection. Producers laughed at him, saying it would never make a good movie, especially with him playing the lead; however, yet again, Sylvester Stallone persevered until he found one producer who wanted the script. The problem was they didn't want him as the lead. They even went as far as to offer him $225,000 to use the script providing he wasn't in the movie. Again, Sylvester Stallone knew exactly want he wanted; he wanted to be a successful actor at all costs … so rejected the deal despite being dead broke. Eventually, the producers agreed to buy the script and let him play the lead actor but only for $35,000.

The movie *Rocky*, written by and starring Sylvester Stallone, was released in 1976 and went on to gross $225 million at the global box office. The movie won three Oscars for best picture, best directing, and best film editing. Sylvester Stallone was nominated for best actor. Rocky was also entered into the American National Film Registry as one of the greatest movies ever.

The rest, as they say, is history. The Rocky franchise has since produced another five films alone whilst Sylvester Stallone has acted in a number of other blockbusters.

Have you ever wondered why some people win while others don't? If you think the reason has anything to do with luck, privilege, or God loving them more, you're wrong. Dead wrong. And let me say this: some people are born into wealthy, connected families, and as a result, things are given to them without them having to work hard for it (hold on to that last phrase!). However, that doesn't automatically make them successful. It's so important that you realize that a person can have enough money to buy houses and land, go to the best schools, and own businesses—but that alone does not automatically make him a successful person.

Two primary things separate those who win from those who don't: mindset and actions. They are the topics I pretty much address throughout this book because they are essential to whether you succeed or fail, and I cannot stress enough how important it is to think positively about your life (your present and your future) and to act on those thoughts. Sylvester Stallone wasn't born with a silver spoon in his mouth. You read his story. He certainly wasn't lucky, because producers initially scorned his idea, laughed at him and told him he didn't have a good story. Remember that? And I know God doesn't love him more than He loves you or me. After believing God only favored the nation of Israel, the apostle Peter came to realize God loves everyone equally. He said to Cornelius, a non-Jewish man seeking salvation, "I now realize how true it is that God does not show favoritism but accepts from every nation the one who fears him and does what is right."[24] So if your neighbor, your friend, your cousin, or your high school or college classmate is winning, but you are not, you cannot point to luck or favoritism on God's part. And neither can you point to your religious beliefs as the reason.

I am amazed by the number of people who think Christians, or those who believe in God, are not to be successful during their time on earth but are to wait until they arrive on the other side, in the new life, wherever you believe it to be. And then there are those who believe they will never be successful because of where they live. When it comes to winning in life, where you live or what religion you practice doesn't matter. Even where and how you were born doesn't

---

[24] Acts 10:34-35, NIV

matter. What is important is where you're going *if* you put in the time and effort. That's right! The difference between winning and not winning is action.

As a minister, I meet and interact with many people almost daily. I often talk to others about their lives and the problems they are grappling with. One of the most perplexing things I've discovered is many people believe success and prosperity are reserved for those who live on the right side of the street, have the "right" skin color, possess academic degrees, or have the right human connections. Now, I am not naïve to believe that factors such as location, race and ethnicity, education, and whom you know don't ever play a role in how readily some opportunities are available to certain people. It's true that some people, based on those very things, may have to work even harder than their counterparts. But I do believe the sky is the limit for anyone of any background when they set their hearts and minds and hands and feet toward winning and don't give up when they encounter challenges.

When people cannot see past the limitations they have set for themselves, they often make excuses for not pursuing a goal or not pressing past the obstacles that sometimes get in the way. They may say things such as "It's not time," "I tried, but nothing ever good happens for me," or "I don't have what it takes to succeed at that." One great example of this is a young man who applied to become a police officer in his city but failed the physical fitness test by a hair—he was only seconds off the required time for a one-mile run. He thought he had lost his opportunity, but a few months later, the police department gave him another chance to take the test. He had a couple of months to train for it, but practically every day he would make an excuse for not going to the gym until a week leading up to the test. That week, he found his way to the gym, and he felt pretty good about his chances when the day of the second test arrived, but once again he fell short. And the second failure sunk his confidence even further. But guess what happened? The police department gave him an unprecedented third opportunity to take the test. He thought to himself, *this time, I'm going to get a personal trainer and work hard to ensure I past that test.* But just as he had done before, he procrastinated, and this time he never made it to the gym. When the day of the test arrived, he didn't even bother to take the test because he knew he wasn't ready for it.

Whether you tell yourself you don't have what it takes to succeed at something you're trying to achieve—lose weight, get out of debt, buy your first house, or launch a business—or you procrastinate, fear and doubt are the likely culprits behind your refusal or delay to move.

If you are one of those people who doesn't strive to prosper in this life because you believe everything good is on the other side, let me say this: you were not born to only live a sinless, pure life on earth in preparation for eternity someplace else. And you weren't born to live a mediocre life. What is a mediocre life, you ask? It is an average, ordinary, undistinguished, indifferent, unexceptional, and unremarkable way of living. It's living safely.

Stallone knew what he wanted out of life, and he chose to win at all costs. And if he could press through multiple rejections to realize his dream of becoming an actor, I know you can overcome any obstacle that gets in your way. What do you think—can you do it?

We are born to succeed in all aspects of life. Jesus said, "I have come that you may have life, and have it to the full."[25] The New Living Translation and Holman Christian Standard Bible translations of Jesus' promise read:

"My purpose is to give them a rich and satisfying life." (NLT)

"I have come so that they may have life and have it in abundance." (NIV)

The Greek translation for the word "abundance" means overflow. We are born to live life in the overflow.

I don't believe in accidents or coincidence. Some things may appear to occur by chance, but nothing does. For instance, even if your parents didn't plan to conceive you when they came together, you were not conceived by accident. You were made purposefully. If you don't believe me, believe these words penned by David in Psalm 139: "For You formed my innermost parts; You knit me [together] in my mother's womb. I will give thanks and praise to You, for I am fearfully and wonderfully made; Wonderful are Your works, and my soul knows it very well."[26] There's so much good stuff in those verses! First, although your parents conceived you, you were created by God. Thus, your life is not a mistake—even if you were raised by parents who adopted you. That's right: you were born on purpose. As a wonderful work of God, you were designed to win. Thus, you will win on purpose just as you were born on purpose. But you must believe that.

---

[25] John 10:10, NIV

[26] Psalm 139:13-14, Amplified Bible

You are the master of your fate. Our Creator has given us something called choice, and He won't interfere with our decision. In fact, He honors it. Whatever choice you make, He will honor it. Did you know for Him to work in your life, He needs your cooperation? Winning is a choice that you must make, and He doesn't want you to settle for anything less than the best. Professional development author Jeffrey Gitomer wrote in an article published on Success.com, "There is no prize in sales for second place. It's win or nothing. The masters know this and strive for—they fight for—that winning edge."[27]

I have heard so many people say things such as, "I'm waiting on God to bless me" and "I'm waiting for the right time for God to move in my life." Listen, we must understand that God doesn't move past our will. If you do nothing and wait for God to bless you, you will be waiting for a very long time. However, if you choose to pursue winning, God will honor that. He will fuel the fight and effort you put into winning with unbelievable power and strength. The author of the book of Revelation wrote, "Behold, I stand at the door and knock. If anyone hears My voice and opens the door, I will come in to him and dine with him, and he with Me."[28] The author is saying God needs someone to open the door for Him to enter? Yes, because the choice is yours to make.

If you're wondering why God doesn't just break down the door down and come in, it's because He's God. He could do that if He wanted to. He could walk through the door if He wanted to because He can do anything! But He chooses not to.

---

[27] http://www.success.com/article/jeffrey-gitomer-the-ten-traits-of-high-sales-performers

[28] Revelation 3:20, NKJV

He allows you to choose because He wants you to want it. God is sovereign, meaning He is self-governing and confers with no one.

This book is full of information, motivation, and instruction on how you can be truly successful in your endeavors, but no one is going to put a gun to your head and force you to apply what you're reading. It's your decision to make. The application of anything I share with you is only effective if you want to succeed. Since you are reading it, don't stop at underlining passages that jump out at you or taking notes. Apply what I'm saying and take it all the way to a street named just for you: Success Boulevard.

Whether you believe in God or not, if you don't decide to do what it takes to be a winner, it will not happen for you. You have a choice to make between life and death, prosperity and poverty. In the book of Deuteronomy, the author writes, "Now listen, today I am giving you a choice between life and death, prosperity and disaster." It's your choice.

Decide to be a winner—choose life—and expect God to come to your aid.

You've Got Potential

Born with the ability to become something special, you can accomplish great things in your life. I truly believe that because of a declaration made by the writer of Psalm 139: "Thank you for making me so wonderfully complex! Your workmanship is marvelous—how well I know it."[29] The writer is thanking God for creating him and making him special. And because God created us, that sentiment also applies to us. It means we can do anything we put our minds to and go as far as our minds can think. However, not everyone will tap into their ability. So, it's up to you. Are you ready to become one of the ones who do or the many who don't?

We're constantly growing; no one stays in one place for any period. Some of our capabilities remain undeveloped and hidden until circumstances are suitable for their emergence. Our objective is to tap into those hidden abilities and develop them; we are to seek and create circumstances conducive for unearthing our hidden abilities.

The mustard seed is one of the smallest plant seeds. It measures about 0.039 to 0.079 inches in diameter, yet it has great growth potential. Jesus said the mustard seed "is the smallest of all seeds on earth. When planted, however, it grows and becomes the largest of all garden plants, with such big branches that the birds can perch in its shade."[30] He was likening the Kingdom of God to a mustard seed. He also likened it to our faith. Even if our faith is as small as a mustard seed, with it we could do incredible things; we can move mountains![31] Faith grows. When you choose to believe in yourself and your dreams and begin to act on that belief, your faith will simply grow from there. Faith that starts out the size of a mustard seed will grow.

---

[29] Psalm 139:14, NLT
[30] Mark 4, The Parable of the Sower
[31] Matthew 17:20

Don't despise small beginnings. You must start somewhere; there is always the potential of doing something extraordinary, such as a becoming the top candidate for a senior-level position for a well-respected company, gaining a coveted spot on a board, starting a nonprofit that serves disenfranchised populations, turning your passion into a business, and so on. When you nurture that small beginning with practice, continued development, relationship building, and so on, you will grow from being someone who has the potential to becoming someone who has arrived.

We all came into this world with no clue how to perform or articulate an idea. We had no idea. Everything we know now, we had to learn. We were born neither with the will to win, the desire to succeed, nor the urge to reach our full potential; we had to develop these traits. We came into this world with a blank slate, and the potential to go either direction. Where we go is up to us. Let's face it: anything worth having will have ups and downs. There will be good days and bad days. You will have gains and losses. That's life. However, the challenge is not to abort your dreams or ditch your goals in the dry or fiery seasons of your life. Unfortunately, that's exactly what some people do. They lose their focus and end up questioning whether they were on the right track to make their dream come true or whether they wanted the wrong thing altogether.

I will tell you this: no one or nothing can stop you from reaching your full potential—I don't care what happens. The challenge is to recognize your dream, pursuing a course that reflects who you truly are; **and** develop the skills you need to fulfill your dream, exhibiting character and leadership from start to finish. During the process, you must be open to making necessary adjustments when needed.

Dormant Potential

Read any story in the Bible about Jesus, and it becomes clear that He's all about wanting people to live their lives to the fullest. And most of those stories we read about Him touching people and performing miracles inspire us, right? He heals people left and right (e.g., the blind and the disabled); He gives people second chances (e.g., the adulterous woman); He shows love for people society tosses away (e.g., the woman at the well and the tax collector). I can fill this page with examples of the tender loving ways in which Jesus helped people to demonstrate lessons about unconditional love, grace, and mercy. But there's a story in the Bible about Jesus that may not leave you with warm fuzzies.

One day when Jesus was leaving Bethany, a town he often visited during his earthly ministry, he became hungry. He saw a fig tree from a distance, and because it bore leaves, he may have assumed it had fruit. Although it was fig season, the fruit generally grew before the leaves. When he reached the tree and saw there was no fruit, just the leaves, he did something we never saw him do before: He pronounced death to a thing instead of life. "May no one ever eat fruit from you again," he said as he cursed the tree.[32] Sounds harsh, doesn't it? Especially since the writer tells us it was not the season for figs. So why would Jesus curse a tree for not being ready to produce? There's a deeper, theological meaning that has more to do with what He saw in Israel at the time—a profession of faith but no fruit. But I think it speaks to what can happen if

---

[32] Mark 11:12-14, 20-21

we allow our potential to lie dormant. For instance, if we're constantly talking about our dreams and goals but don't move one inch toward fulfilling them, we can be like that fig tree—growing leaves (all talk) but producing no fruit (an action that backs up the talk). The consequences for not living up to our potential can be costly. When we're not doing anything to work toward our goals, our potential will lie dormant, meaning it will remain hidden and undeveloped. It could be laziness that holds us back, but most likely it's fear. The bottom line is we'll eventually lose it if we don't use it, and there's nothing that turns off people more than someone who is all talk and no action.

Whether you're afraid of failing or succeeding, you must take a risk. Both failure and success require change. Change is something most people tend to avoid at all costs because it isn't easy to do, can hurt, and often costs us something we think we cannot part with. Some people worry about how success will affect them, and there are those who are afraid people will treat them differently after they become successful. If you risk nothing, you'll achieve nothing.

Let's stop here for a moment. I want you to identify some of the things you know you need to change in your life, and write them in your journal or in the space below:

If you haven't made a move to begin making these changes in your life, what's holding you back? If today were your last opportunity to make a move toward your dream, would you go for it today? Are you ready to face your fears head on?

What's Holding You Back?

Everyone wants to be fulfilled—we all would like answers to life's "whys." The answers are what will keep us going, or so we tell ourselves. However, for some of us, finding fulfillment is not easy. Sometimes, we're not clear about what we are meant to do with our lives. If you feel stuck and are uncertain about what to do, you may be doing something that is hindering you from figuring things out. Here are five things that could be possibly making it difficult for you to identify your purpose and reach your full potential

1. You don't set aside time to reflect on your potential

The fast-paced lifestyle people maintain today is not conducive to reflection. When was the last time you set aside time to just meditate on who you are and what you want to do with your potential? If you're like many people today, your daily planner is filled with tasks. You barely have time to eat.

It's important you set aside time to think things through and figure them out. Sometimes, it is a time of reflection that allows you to clear your mind and focus on what you are trying to accomplish.

2. You don't pay attention to your feelings

While you ought to think logically about achieving your goals in life, it's also important to listen to what your gut instincts tell you. The Christian faith teaches us that God can also speak to us through our feelings. If you are feeling dissatisfied and restless, pay attention to that. It might be God's way of telling you there are greater things ahead or in store for you.

Some people call it intuition, or "woman's intuition," something every woman seems to possess. It's uncanny how accurate a woman's gut feeling is when it tells her that her lover is two-timing her or that a co-worker cannot be trusted although she has no concrete evidence of either. She just knows, and she's often right. It's that gut feeling that something is wrong. It may come in the form of a dream, *déjà vu*, a funny feeling, all three, or something else. And these are not feelings restricted only to women. The point is—whether you're a woman or a man—when it comes to making moves to meet your goals and living your dreams, never doubt that feeling. Ever. It just might be the key to unlocking your unfulfilled potential.

3. You let your friends or family decide for you

Do you have a difficult time making a decision and often find yourself asking anyone who'll listen what you should do? If you are indecisive, it can be tempting to go with what your friends and family think you should do, which may not be the right decision for you. Many people have taken on a profession or goal in life because that was what was expected of them. While the advice of others may be right in some instances, always seeking and following it can lead to stagnation in your growth and cause you to settle for something contrary to where God is leading you.

4. You are afraid to make mistakes or change

The perfectionist in you likely wants to get it right the first time. As a result, you don't make room for error. Although they are a part of growth and success, you find them to be paralyzing. Change is hard for most people, let alone a stickler for excellence. However, if you have discerned your passion and find that you are on the wrong path toward fulfilling your goals based on new information or new needs, it's important to be open to change and course correct if necessary.

5. You want to be sure *all* the time

People want certainty, which is normal. You want to be sure about a thing before committing to for various reasons, including making sure you can keep your word. As the saying goes, your word is your bond. However, you also need to realize that reaching your destiny will have some uncertainty regarding the details, e.g., how it will pan out, where it will lead you. Always know that despite the risks and uncertainty in going for "it" (and there will be many twists and turns along the way) God is with you every step of the way. The journey toward fulfilling your purpose will be worth every bead of sweat on your brow, every tear that forms in your eye, every moment of triumph, and every moment of disappointment over the setbacks you will inevitably experience along the way. Just knowing you are on the right path, and that you're moving toward inevitable victory in your life will leave you with the peace and joy that comes with discovering who you are and what you are meant to do.

Overcoming the Fear of Dissatisfaction

Isn't it interesting that although we were not given a spirit of fear,[33] we still insist on adopting it? Fear is most prevalent and paralyzing when we remain focused on our shortcomings and what we deem to be "reality." I love the way Dr. Charles Stanley explains it:

> "Fear focuses our attention on ourselves and on things we do not need to consider. It fills our minds with hypothetical situations that all end in defeat and ruination. Eventually, it utterly consumes us. Therefore we cannot shrink back in obeying God and using the gifts He has given us because He is ultimately in control of our futures, and we are never victims of our circumstances."[34]

---

[33] 2 Timothy 1:7

[34] Stanley, Charles F., Ed. Life Principles Bible. Nashville: Thomas Nelson, 2009, p. 1469, explanation of 2 Timothy 1:7

If reality shows God's presence, we will understand that we all were born with a sound mind, with no fear in sight. So where did fear come from, and why does it linger in our minds?

There's an acronym for fear that's popular among Christians. It spells out fear this way: False Evidence Appearing Real. I like to put it another way: Fear is only a fake Emotion that appears to be real. When a baby first exits its mother's womb, it typically signals that he or she is okay by crying loudly. His pattern of crying whenever he has a need pretty much continues in the initial days and months of the baby's life. Just ask any sleepless new parent. As the child begins to grow, it learns to crawl without fear. Then the baby starts standing, sometimes falling on shaky legs, but he continues to try, at times taking a step or two before he falls again but never giving up until eventually, he is walking with confidence and at "infant speed" pace. Then suddenly, you're the one afraid of all the things your baby will get into now that he can walk. Notice though, how that child, with no real knowledge of the sting of failure, naturally keeps getting up and trying to walk until he masters it.

Where does the fear come from that we adults try to hold on to so badly? And how can we get rid of it? Do you see what I'm getting at? The anxiety and apprehension caused by the presence or anticipation of danger are not in your DNA; it's not in your makeup. Whatever that thing is that makes you so afraid of failing that you quit trying or never try at all was never a part of God's plan for your life.

To overcome fear, you must understand that everyone has two options they can exercise in life, faith or fear. The one you choose to embrace is up to you—God won't force you to trust Him or use the gift He has given you. But please just remember that one of these was given to you and the other one you adopted on your own.

Hopefully, by now, you want to know how to get rid of your fear. And I'm eager to tell you how. Following is a three-step process for crushing fear in your life. I call it the "Triple A Program." The three steps are simple: Analyze, Attitude, and Actions. Let's review them.

Analyze your situation and make a decision. How do you perceive your life? Your first attack against fear is to take an honest inventory of where you are and how you tend to respond to various situations, good or bad. Does your response tend to be led by a fear that the worst will happen if it's bad or it won't last for long if it's good? What makes you respond the way you do? Can you point to a time in your life, say your childhood, teenage years, and so on where fear began to creep in and make you more hesitant? The point is to develop a process of reasoning before you react; either your faith is going to lead the way, or your fear is going to paralyze you.

Examine Your Attitude. Your attitude will impact your decision. Do you have an arrogant or assertive approach to certain situations? Do you find yourself moving forward on opportunities or retreating? Are you talking about what you want to do, or are you constantly talking about what you used to do? Are you ruing on past mistakes, things you cannot change, or are you talking about ways you can go about meeting your goals differently to ensure success?

Don't get mired in hypothetical musings such as "What if this happens" or "This may not work out," no matter whose voice it is, either yours or someone else's. Such are the attributes of the unbeliever.

How do you carry yourself when you walk out of your house? Is your head always up, or are your eyes planted on the ground? Are your shoulders squared or are they rounded? Your posture tells a lot about your mindset, which I'll explain a bit more toward the end of the book.

Take action. Taking action is the "granddaddy" of the Triple-A program. To overcome the kind of fear that paralyzes you and keeps you from pursuing your dreams, you must act quickly and aggressively before fear realizes what you are trying to accomplish. That way, there is no time to concentrate on the fear of failure. It takes as much energy to worry as it does to believe in yourself. If you haven't done something before, of course, it's easy to think that it can't be done. And I realize it can be difficult to go beyond your comfort zone, but you must have enough faith in yourself to give it a go.

God created you to have power. You were not created to escape life by daydreaming, window shopping, playing video games all day, or surfing social media for hours. You were made to achieve greatness in the earth. Often when you find yourself miserable in your job or your day-to-day life, feeling like something is missing but you can't seem to pinpoint what, it's likely because you are confused or clueless about what you are created to be and do. God makes sure we understand that achievement is a vital part of who we are. And don't despise where you are today if you're making moves to grow. Whether you're working the night shift or day shift, in an office cubicle or the comfort of your home, it's not your final destination. Don't think you've missed your purpose or that you're not using your power. You are right where you should be, so continue to work in excellence until it's time for you to move.

Exercising Power in Your Life

Abraham Lincoln said, "Nearly all men can stand adversity, but if you want to test a man's character, gives him power."[35] While one's character comprises his or her distinctive mental and moral qualities, one's power can be defined as his or her ability to dictate how others act or influence the outcome of an event.

When you can speak and expect an immediate result, you have power. Jesus had power and then some. He could influence people, control nature, and perform extraordinary acts, miracles to be exact. He could turn water into wine. He could stop a fierce windstorm with a simple command. He could take a couple of fish and five loaves of bread and multiply them into enough to feed thousands, with leftovers to boot. He had what. He Jesus wasn't just powerful. He had what I call supernatural power.

Then there is personal power, which is a source of influence and authority a person has over others, particularly those who follow him or her. People like teachers, police officers, and pastors can influence and control others.

To possess power is a good and excellent thing, but it will be challenged. Power is fabulous, but caution the one who has such ability. And power without character can be a dangerous thing. I know you want power, even if possessing it would change you. But if you are certain you want it, you must first modify the way you think (mainly about yourself) and then be prepared for the changes it will bring about in your life,

---

[35] https://brainyquote/a/abrahamlin101343.html

including more responsibility, adjustments in your relationships, greater demand for time, and so on.

You have the potential to acquire power just by changing your mindset. It will be a waste to see such power and abilities go to waste because you don't believe in yourself or you continue to allow fear to get in the way. You can change your mindset beginning today, right now, and command success in your life. Yes, power is there for the taking. As Nike says, "Just do it," and as Carl Mathis says, "Go get it."

Open the Eyes of Your Mind

To reach the end of your journey toward success, you need a **vision**. A vision is an act or power of seeing. More importantly, a vision is the act or power of imagination. It's what you see in your mind about your future, beyond the naked eye.

Chuck Swindoll said in "*Living Above the Level of Mediocrity*" about developing a vision,

> "Vision is the ability to see God's presence, to perceive God's power, to focus on God's plan in spite of the obstacles."
>
> "Vision is the ability to see above and beyond the majority."
>
> "Vision is perception, reading the presence and power of God into one's circumstances."

Have you ever wondered what insight you could gain when you're thinking aligns with the same vision God has for your life? To see your vision come alive right before your eyes is to witness a marvelous sight.

We often see things as they are in the present. However, according to the Bible, we should envision the future as if it were the present. So, what does it mean to have a vision? It is painting a picture in your mind of accomplishing all that you have set in your heart to pursue. In other words, having a vision is seeing yourself as a winner.

Meditate on the following questions for a moment. Then give an honest answer to each one.

Can you see your future?

If yes, do you see yourself being different from who you are today?

If so, how?

From the following adjectives, choose how you see yourself in the future and share a brief statement explaining why you see yourself that way.

A: Successful

B: Wealthy

C: Prosperous

D: Victorious

E: All the above

Choose one of the following statements that best describes how you see yourself in the future, and then share a brief statement about why you see yourself that way.

A: I'm confident about my life

B: I speak with boldness.

C: My attitude and my focus are steadfast.

D: I will never quit until I win.

E: All the above

Remember this: "Vision is the ability to see above and beyond the majority." ~Chuck Swindoll

You must see your future before you can acquire it. Envision it as though it has already happened. Paint a picture of your intentions, or impending goal, in your mind. Then think like the winner you are, and act as though you won.

The Power of Focusing

Are you ready to figure out what really matters to you and how to create an extraordinary life? Here are four more exercises you need to complete.

1: Write out your life's vision.

In Scripture it is written, "Write the vision and make it plain."

Don't anticipate a clear, perfect, and well-defined vision overnight.; it takes time to form. So, don't worry if you think nothing's happening. Spend as much time as you need creating it. It may take one hour, several days, or even several weeks.

First, start thinking about your dreams, hopes, and goals, as well as your values in life. Ask yourself what you want and why you want it. Be honest with yourself and remember that it is okay to dream big. The bigger the dream, the better it is.

Be sure to focus on your aspirations, not what others expect of you or what you think you should do. If you feel stuck, ask yourself, "How can I serve?"

When you focus only on what you *want, and* not on what you don't want, you will get exactly what you want.

Be sure you consider all the areas of your life: romantic relationships, friendships, family, career, personal growth, hobbies, health, quality of life, and so on. You will be amazed at how all areas of our life connect; they're linked like a chain, as one impacts the other.

After you've listed the most important things, add details.

Your vision should include measurable results you are going to achieve in your life and when.

Finally, relax and make the exercise fun. You can always change, add, or remove something later.

2: Make a list of things you love to do.

Following are some of the questions to consider when compiling a list of the things you like to do:

What does your ideal day look like?

Who are you spending it with?

What are you doing?

When have you been happiest in your life?

What makes you feel alive and invigorated?

Write down everything that comes to mind—whether it's something minimal like reading a good book or working on the house or something big like traveling around the world or writing books.

The purpose is to make the list as long as possible. I suggest thinking of 101 things if you can. After you're done, go through your list and rank your favorite things from one to 101 (or as far as your list goes). That way, you will be able to narrow it down to the things you love to do and won't leave out anything.

3: Write down all your talents and interests.

The goal of this step is to help you to get an even better idea of who you are. Foremost, write down all the things you're good at or are knowledgeable about. Remember, you don't have to be an expert or gifted, just good at these things. Don't be reluctant. Try to come up with as many things as possible. Talk to your friends and coworkers to ask them what you should put on that list. Ask them for feedback about areas in which they believe you're good at. Their answers may astonish you.

____
____
____
____
____

4. List your genuine passions and principles. Compile everything you listed in the previous steps, but also add things that are important to you.

For example, friendships, health, spiritually, fitness, love, and so on. If you know your ideals, you know what you want, you know who you are, and you know where you stand in life.

After you have completed all four steps, review what you have written daily to help you remain focused and moving confidently toward your goals.

Now let's move on to how you become a winner.

Chapter Four: Becoming a Winner

"You were born to win, but to be a winner, you must plan to win, prepare to win, and expect to win."

~Zig Ziglar

At age 16, while most boys his age were probably learning how to drive, Frank Abagnale Jr. was passing bad checks. By twenty-one, he was a seasoned con man. He had written $2.5 million in fraudulent checks and had successfully posed as an airline pilot, a doctor, a lawyer, and a professor. Abagnale's crimes eventually caught up with him, and he spent five years in a federal prison before being released and employed by the U.S. government as a forgery and document theft expert. Today, that former imposter runs his own agency, which teaches financial institutions, big businesses, and law enforcement how to detect and protect themselves against fraud.[36] Abagnale was so crafty, and his story so intriguing, that he became the subject of a Hollywood movie starring big name actors Leonardo DiCaprio and Tom Hanks. Despite a troubling beginning in his life, he was able to turn it around—thanks in part to receiving a second chance—and become a winner.

---

[36] https://www.biography.com/people/frank-abagnale-20657335

Like Abagnale, you were born to win, but you weren't born a winner.

Abagnale's story is the perfect example that while we were born with certain gifts there is no guarantee that we'll go on to use those gifts or lead successful lives. As Zig Ziglar's quote suggests, no one is born with the idea of wanting to win. When you exited your mother's womb, the doctor simply declared, "It's a girl" or "It's a boy," and nothing more. We all enter this world with a clean slate, having no ideas, no belief, no confidence—just skin and bones. Everything about who we are and what we could accomplish we have to learn, develop, and work at with diligence. And it all starts with the mind.

The mind works this way: the unconscious mind continuously communicates with the conscious mind via the subconscious. This process provides us with meaning to all our interactions with the world. Then it's filtered through our beliefs and habits. Finally, it communicates through our emotions, imagination, sensations, and dreams.

The ability of your conscious mind to direct your attention is one of the most remarkable powers you have. Thus, to create the kind of change that leads to success in your life, you must control what you intentionally focus on; the ability to do so is already within you.

Your conscious mind forms thoughts, makes decisions, and chooses an action. It is also the one that absorbs information, stores it, and then decides whether to act on it or reject it altogether. When the conscious mind decides to take action, the subconscious mind takes over. To put it another way, whatever you dwell on is what you will act on. If you train your thoughts on being a winner by reciting affirmations such as "I am a winner" and visualize yourself as such, your conscious mind will take action, and your unconscious mind will accept it as truth and reality. As long as you continue to do that, it will become nearly impossible for a depressing thought to crawl into the crevices of your mind. So, one of the keys to success is to take full control of your conscious mind and remain focused on what you want to accomplish. That is the beginning stage of attaining any level of success.

A person can be physically imprisoned, trapped in inhumane conditions but still be free in his or her mind. Biblical history provides an excellent example of this fact. The books of Ephesians, Philippians, Colossians, and Philemon are often called the prison epistles. They were written by the apostle Paul during his first imprisonment in Rome. Yet nothing about the letters hint at depression, self-pity, or bitterness. Paul used words like "joy," "hope," and "love" to express his frame of mind in his letters. How was he able to do that, even when he knew his execution was imminent? Because he knew the outcome of his situation: eternity in God's presence. In Paul's mind, he had already won despite being behind prison walls—his physical imprisonment was only temporary and short-term, unlike his victory.

Remember, your conscious mind has the power to direct your attention and awareness toward creating change in your life. That's why it's important to control what you consciously focus on. That is also an excellent example of why you should never say, "I'm going to be a winner," but instead say, "I am a winner." Saying it the latter way means you have made up in your mind that you are already a winner. Nothing beats a made-up mind.

Whatever you put into your mind is what you'll get out of it. If you say you're going to be a winner (future tense), you're essentially accepting that you are not a winner (present tense).

However, when you speak what is to be, you are more likely to act on your belief, following the steps toward manifesting victory and success in your life.

In Christendom, you are taught to believe you have already received victory, not that you are going to receive it. So, trust that you already have it. A Scripture that has become somewhat of an adage among Christians is to speak those things that are not as though they were. The way you do that is to act like its already so, dress like it's already so, speak like it's already so. Once again drawing from Christendom, we are taught that if you are poor and you desire to be rich, act like you're rich; if you are weak, act like you are strong; and so on. The objective is to act like what you desire to be and not acquiesce to your current situation. That is how you activate your faith. By claiming success now, you encourage yourself to live at the level you want to be.

I get that it may be difficult for you to say your life is a bed of roses if you seem to be staring down problems on every side; however, even during your challenges, you must have a mind to win. If you want to be a winner, you must choose to smell the roses and see the silver linings in tough situations as signs of imminent victory. Remember, you must speak *and think* those things that are not as though they are.

Now I want to ask you directly: Do you have the mind to win? I want you to answer in the space below, and not just in your head.

In the book of Romans, one of those prison letters, Paul instructed his readers to "be transformed by the renewal of your mind." His instructions were for its readers back then, as well as for its readers today, including us. Renewing our minds cannot be a one-time thing; we must do it daily because we're up against so much, and we don't know what life will bring our way on any given day. Our actions are the result of our thinking. I have heard people make statements such as "I wish I could do this all over again" and "I made a grave mistake; I will never do this again." But guess what? If their minds are not renewed, they will keep making the same choices and getting the same results, no matter how much they don't want to.

Whether you win or lose is the result of how you think. If you think you will win, you are right. If you think you will lose, you are correct again. So, guess what? You are always right. The decisions you make are always right, your manifestation is always right, and the mistakes you make are always right. Your thoughts transpire into action. So, if you're tired of what you're getting, change the way you think to get the result you want. That is why you must continually renew your mind. Think of the renewal process as software regularly used to detect and clean viruses in a computer or rid it of old files that are slowing it down. Negative thoughts can build up and take up space in our minds like old files, or become viruses that compromise our belief systems when we download erroneous information. Thus, we must regularly sweep our minds for negative thoughts that can set us up for failure. Right thinking leads to blessings and abundant living.

I love the Olympic Games because they place the will to win on full display. They are a grand demonstration of the sacrifices people make to fulfill their dreams, cross the finish line, and realize victory. Perhaps you witnessed the courageous event that took place in the 1992 Barcelona Olympics.

> "Twenty-four years ago, British sprinter Derek Redmond and his father provided audiences with one of the most heart-wrenching, goose bump-inducing moments in Olympic history. At the 1992 Barcelona Olympics, Redmond had qualified for the semifinal of the 400m with the fastest time in his heat. He was looking strong when suddenly he pulled up—his hamstring had torn. Rather than crumble to the ground, Redmond continued hobbling toward the finish line. Surprisingly, he didn't have to finish the race alone. However, Redmond's father, Jim, ran from the stands and brushed off security to join his son. With tears in both of their eyes, the Redmond's finished the race together."[37]

As sports journalist Colin Ward-Henninger concluded in his column about Olympian Derek Redmond, the runner's will to finish the race triumphed "over injury that should have been impossible to overcome."[38]

---

[37] https://www.cbssports.com/olympics/news/watch-when-an-injured-olympians-father-helped-him-cross-the-finish-line/

[38] ibid

What life offers is there for anyone who has enough guts to take it. My question to you is, do you who want it, and if so, how much do you want it? When it comes to being successful, the biggest struggle most people have is the fear of failure. No one wants to fail, but once you get over the fear of life defeating you by conditioning your mind to think like a winner, every other step will fall into place. Have you ever said the following things to yourself?

There's got to be a better way.

Why am I not as successful as my friends?

What are they doing that I am not?

They seem to have it all together.

I wish my life were like theirs.

If you've ever asked yourself those questions, or some form of them, what you need to do is take your eyes of other people, especially that one person you're often comparing yourself to, and begin putting the desires of your heart in motion.

Success can be defined or categorized in many ways, depending on the individual. The same thing can be said about almost anything in life, but it's how you perceive life to be and how you attack it that will determine how successful you will be. You can accomplish anything you desire when you put your mind to it.

How to Handle Challenges

"I want to be successful, but I have a few situations I need to handle." Does this sound like you?

Let me simplify what I'm trying to get at. What you think about most will eventually be the dominant force in your mind. It will determine which direction you take, or whether you will accept the situation and move forward with your life. As we know, children can cause you to lose your cool sometimes. Your spouse rattles your nerves every occasionally. Your job frustrates you from time to time, and so on. But the question is how do you handle it? Here's how:

1. Choose something that makes you smile, and think about it every day. By thinking about it, you will program it into your mind, which will transform into action, and as a result, your attitude toward that situation will change.
2. Realize that you are not the only one dealing with trials, so don't be so hard on yourself. In many cases, your problem may be small compared to someone else's.

Everyone grapples with challenging situations at points in their lives. So, when you're facing one yourself, you must decide that it's all up to you and only you to work your way through it and come out of it shining. You can change any situation you want or need to change; all you must do is use it to your advantage.

Here is how this works.

A thought is a seed planted in your mind by an event, something you were told, or something you witnessed or experienced. Just like any living thing, it needs food and water to grow. Concerning the mind, whatever you feed your thought allows it to linger and fester in your mind. It simply continues to grow. So, if the thought is a negative one, it will grow something negative, like weeds. You don't want that to happen.

Therefore, always choose to do something different but positive, something unusual but productive. Be aggressive in growing your brain's ability to think better thoughts that will result in better choices. Make it a habit to constantly examine and change your habits as needed. While you cannot control what happens, you can control how you think and how you respond.

Everything begins with a thought, and the desire of wanting to do something brings that thought into play. If you want to do something bad enough, eventually you will find some way to make it happen.

Ultimately, the only thing that counts is action because action is what makes everything a reality. You can't achieve anything in life without it. Faith (what you believe) without works (action) is dead. So, what you want or believe means nothing if you don't act on it. It's like that fig tree Jesus cursed because it was full of leaves (the appearance of fruitfulness) but no fruit (it wasn't producing anything).

Achievement is the result of your capability and effort. If you want to resolve any situation, act accordingly. However, if you do nothing and wait around, thinking someone is going to come along and give you a handout, chances are you will be waiting a long time. You will be left alone, wondering what happened. Have you ever imagined winning a large sum of money, thinking that would instantly solve a bunch of problems in your life? Well, some people really think that way. They sit around doing nothing except wishing and hoping and buying lottery tickets, looking to win that elusive jackpot. If you play the Powerball lottery and you're looking to win the grand prize, your chances are 1 in 292, 201, 338; but if you're willing to settle for a $4 jackpot, you have a 1 in 32 chances of winning.[39] The point: don't place your hope for financial freedom and riches in playing the lottery. If you take that gamble often, you may end up spending more money buying tickets than you'll ever win.

You are not bound by your thoughts or your way of thinking. In fact, the choice you make is the critical element in how and what you will think in the future. Choose as you will, and it is inevitable that you will become the person you want to be and live the life you want to live.

Every situation has positive and negative components. Disappointments, setbacks, losses, gains, and wins are all part of life. Purpose, power, and victory are generated by your thoughts. So be optimistic and speak positive, life-giving words, whether you are talking about yourself, others, or your issues. An optimistic attitude and positive talk will enable you to overcome any challenge you may face to enjoy a successful life.

What a Winner Looks Like

When you think about a winner, what image comes to mind? A runner who breaks the ribbon crossing the finish line to stand in gold medal position on the podium? An actor who wins an Academy award? An author who wins a Pulitzer for her envelope-pushing novel? A small business owner who makes six figures his first year in business? No matter how

[39] http://www.powerball.com/powerball/pb_prizes.asp

you define a winner, before you reach that point of becoming one yourself, some conditions must take place in your thinking. I understand that life can be hard; experts say most ventures fail before they get off the ground. Even with that, you must stop feeding yourself self-defeating thoughts. Regardless of the climate, keep pushing toward your dreams and goals. We must keep reminding ourselves that "weeping may endure for a night, but joy comes in the morning." The truth of the matter is that trouble or hardship doesn't last a lifetime: the challenge is to remain focused on the opportunity and not the obstacle during challenging seasons. A winner knows how to "take a licking and keep on ticking." If you encounter one, two, or even three nights of hardship, that doesn't mean the final result will be a failure.

In 1904, *Brown Book Magazine* sponsored a contest for people who could come up with the best answer to the question "What is success?" American writer Bessie Anderson Stanley won that competition, and here's how she defined a successful person:

He has achieved success who has lived well, laughed often, and loved much;
Who has enjoyed the trust of pure women, the respect of intelligent men and the love of little children;
Who has filled his niche and accomplished his task;
Who has never lacked appreciation of Earth's beauty or failed to express it;
Who has left the world better than he found it,
Whether an improved poppy, a perfect poem, or a rescued soul;
Who has always looked for the best in others and given them the best he had;

Whose life was an inspiration;
Whose memory a benediction.[40]

These main three characteristics of a successful person according to Stanley—to live well, laugh often, and love much—should give you a sense of someone who has achieved something priceless in his or her lifetime, something better than riches and accolades. And it's something we should aspire to achieve.

Besides having a positive outlook and a good work ethic, another trait that defines a true winner in life is giving back. Strive to make a positive contribution to society. When it's all said and done, be someone whom others can say lived a life of quality and value. What does living a life of quality and value mean? It's a basic question, yet it's not easy to define because there's no one definitive answer. For everyone, life holds a different meaning, and everyone has a different way of living. No matter what you try to do with yours, it's always good to remember that it will not last forever; thus, it is imperative you focus on what matters most—living well, laughing often, and loving much. And if I can add to Stanley's definition, it is also loving and respecting your unique, God-given life.

Because we all start off on the same page, we pretty begin our journey wanting to live a life worth remembering, something to be proud of. As parents care for their children, take care of your life with the tender care, unconditional love, and respect it deserves, such as make wise decisions and walk a path of happiness and fulfillment. Our earthly lives are not meant to last forever. We're on a temporary sojourn, so we

---

[40] https://en.wikipedia.org/wiki/Bessie_Anderson_Stanley

must make the most of every minute we receive on Earth. You must also understand that true winners take care of themselves. They maintain a healthy balance physically, spiritually, and emotionally. Winners find true balance and learn how not to overextend themselves. They enjoy what life has to offer.

Live a good life until it's your time to move on to the next life. Treasure your time on Earth, and treat it lovingly and respectfully. Live to the best of your ability.

Society tends to gauge the level of one's success by material wealth, social standing, job title, and bank account balances. There is nothing wrong with reaching for the stars and wanting the best the world can offer. It's important, however, to remember that life isn't all about amassing wealth and gaining prestige. Having material things or a pristine reputation doesn't make you a true winner. Place importance on things that are lasting in life such as your relationships with family and friends. Find love and give love whenever and wherever you can. Give back to your community and help those in need. Build yourself to be the kind of person who finds satisfaction in doing more than just acquiring things and status. Include others in your world. If you do all those things, you will become a true winner in life.

Food for Thought

While it's important to reach various levels of accomplishment, you must pay close attention to how you get there. Following are some thoughts I've adapted from others that have helped me in my journey toward attaining success, and I want to share them with you. Write them on index cards or in your journal. Then read them often as a reminder to keep the right perspective in your quest for success.

- The journey is just as important, if not more important, as the destination.
- Your life is your own; live it as you want to live it and be proud.
- Honor the gift of life.
- Honor God by taking care of the life He has given you.
- There is more to life than acquiring material things. Outside of your material possessions, discover what makes life more meaningful for you.
- What's important is not how long you live but how well you live.
- Win at all levels of your life, not just in acquiring possessions.

The final affirmation is about caring for others and rooting for their success as much as you do your own. It's a direct quote by tennis great Venus Williams about her younger sister and sometime competitor, Serena, but you can adapt it where necessary to fit your situation by inserting someone you care about:

> "I always like to win. But I'm the big sister. I want to make sure she has everything, even if I don't have anything. It's hard. I love her too much. That's what counts."[41]

As I studied winners most people are familiar with, I learned most of them share a common trait: they are consistently able to reach ideal levels of accomplishment

---

[41] https://www.brainyquote.com/quotes/quotes/v/venuswilli180892.html

through a combination of confidence, skill, persistence, and hard work. When we think about people like Michael Jordan and the Williams sisters, they will tell you that it's not so much about what they had to work with, but success came about because of the way they think.

Please don't misunderstood what I am trying to get you to understand. Of course, you must work hard, and being talented doesn't hurt. However, it's critical to possess the mindset of a winner before you ever begin winning. Here's what some of those famous winners have said about having the right mindset:

> "Believe in yourself. You've got to take that chance, even if it doesn't make sense. Just believe in yourself. Even if you don't, pretend that you do and at some point, you will. With self-belief comes self-esteem as well. All of those contribute to making good decisions for yourself.... Some people say I have an attitude, maybe I do, but you have to. You have to believe in yourself when no one else does—that makes you a winner right there.... I don't focus on what I'm up against. I focus on my goals, and I try to ignore the rest." ~ Venus Williams

> "Everyone's dreams can come true if you just stick with it and work hard... Since I don't look like every other girl, it takes a while to be okay with that ... but different is good." ~Serena Williams

> "You have to expect things of yourself before you can do them." ~ Michael Jordan

Whether people win or not isn't due to their wealth or power. They win because they made up in their minds who they are and what they can become with hard work and determination. More than talent, skill, and opportunity, desire, action, and determination. I believe success is acquired by exercising a little common sense and using what you have in you. You'll be surprised by what's already inside you if you push yourself to the limit.

Remember, Michael Jordan missed thousands of shots and lost hundreds of games, but he managed to keep going because he didn't focus on his mistakes or losses. His perseverance paid off in more ways than even he probably imagined, as today he is considered the greatest basketball player of all time. He was trusted to take the winning shot about twenty-six times and missed. That could've made him want to give up, but he never did. If your mind is made up to win, you can expect to fall short sometimes, but giving up is not an option.

People who have a winner's mindset live every day as if it were their last. If you possess that type of attitude, you will consistently give your best. Your biggest task is not to get ahead of another person but to surpass your own abilities and achievements. That's how a winning attitude looks.

You Are in Control

Writer James Allen said, "A man sooner or later discovers that he is the master-gardener of his soul, the director of his life."[42] Jackson Kiddard, author and polymath, puts it this way: "Everything you take for granted is a blessing. Everything you fear is a friend in disguise. Everything you

---

[42] https://www.values.com/inspirational-quotes/5884-a-man-sooner-or-later-discovers-that-he-is-the

want is a part of you. Everything you own does not define you. Everything you feel is the only Truth there is to know.

Everything you wish for is already on its way to you. Everything you think creates your life."[43] I cannot say this enough: your thoughts shape your actions. Everything you seek, you will find. Everything you resist will stick around. Everything you release will stay if it's supposed to. Everything you need is right where you are.

Every time you blame another person, you lose your power. Every time you think you can, you can. Every time you fall, you must get up and try again. Every time you cry, you're one tear closer to joy. Every time you ask for forgiveness, all you have to do is forgive yourself.

Everyone you see is your reflection. Everyone you know mirrors you. Everyone wants to be happy. Everyone wants to live in joy. Everyone seeks a higher purpose. Everyone breathes the same breath. Everyone needs love to survive. Everyone has a purpose to fulfill.

Everyone's the same. We just get caught up in the details, such as labels, names, skin color, and religion. We share the same hopes and fears. No one wants to feel the pain life inevitably brings. Everyone's the same as everyone else. Everyone is dying for love to remain.

Who is controlling your life? Who is preventing you from being all you want to be, and who is stopping you from winning in life? Be like that master gardener James Allen alluded to and take control of your destiny.

---

[43] http://thedailylove.com/todays-quotes-perfect-love-casts-out-fear/

Winners Control Their Destiny

I want to share three short stories about some winners you know well and how they didn't allow a setback like getting fired prevent them from pursuing their dreams.

Oprah Winfrey: When One Door Shuts, Another One Will Open

When television mogul and billionaire Oprah Winfrey was just starting out in journalism, one of her first jobs was as a news reporter for a local station in Baltimore; however, she was told by her producer that she was "unfit for television news" because she tended to get emotionally invested in her stories. According to the story, the producer fired her, but he offered her a role on a daytime TV show called *People Are Talking*. Now, how many people do you know are offered another opportunity by the boss who fires them? Not many, I'm sure! I'd like to think he redirected her toward an area that better suited her talents and made room for her passion for connecting with and helping people. With Winfrey's charisma and smarts leading the way, the talk show became a hit. She would go on to host a morning show in Chicago, which gained such popularity with viewers, she was able to start her own talk show, becoming the host of the *Oprah Winfrey Show*, which aired for twenty-five years, ending because she decided it was time. Now she owns her own television network, OWN.[44]

Hillary Clinton: Making Lemonade out of a Lemon

Former Secretary of State Hillary Clinton has to be one of the smartest women out there. When she was running for president of the United States in 2016, two former presidents (her husband and Barack Obama) both admitted that she was much more prepared to be president than they were when they were running. She even has a law degree from Yale. But did you know she was once fired from a job? That's right! Here's the story as told on Businessinsider.com:

> Before heading to Yale, former Secretary of State Hillary Clinton was fired from her brief stint at a salmon cannery in Valdez, Alaska. The former New York Senator on the Today show said that after graduating from Wellesley College, she and some friends worked their way across Alaska washing dishes, and she eventually wound up working in a fishery scooping out salmon guts. She said, "I was given a spoon and some boots and I was told to take out the insides of the salmon." Clinton didn't last long in that role, however, noting that the Japanese workers who were taking out the caviar yelled at her for working too slowly. "So, they literally kicked me out of that job," Clinton said. She says they then placed her on the line packing the salmon head to tail. But when she noticed the salmon was "green and black;

---

[44] https://www.biography.com/people/oprah-winfrey-9534419

> they looked horrible" and a peculiar stench, she questioned the man running the operation about the salmon's quality. "When I left, I came back the next day, and the whole operation was gone," Clinton said. "So, I think that was the equivalent of getting fired."[45]

Clinton told former nighttime talk show host David Letterman that, despite being fired, her short time at the cannery was her "favorite summer job of all time" because it prepared her for working in Washington. She turned what many would view as a negative experience into something positive because it gave her skills she needed for her future job in one of the toughest workplaces out there.

Thomas Edison: The Reward of Never Giving Up

Most people know Thomas Edison as the most prolific inventor in American history, but did you know he was a poor student who struggled in school? He credits his mother for turning him around. She removed him from school after his teacher called him "addled," and taught the young Edison herself. He was a sickly child who lost almost all his hearing by age twelve. But instead of treating his deafness as a handicap, he saw it as an asset because "it made it easier for him to concentrate on his experiments and research."[46] Also, Edison was fired by Western Union after he was caught

---

45 http://www.businessinsider.com/hillary-clinton-reveals-the-time-she-got-fired-2015-10

46 https://www.loc.gov/collections/edison-company-motion-pictures-and-sound-recordings/articles-and-essays/biography/life-of-thomas-alva-edison/

secretly conducting experiments in his office. His firing opened the door for him to pursue his passion. That's when he "decided to pursue inventing full-time and received his first patent two years later for the electric vote recorder."[47]

A true winner isn't easily intimidated by negative experiences such as getting fired or by having to sacrifice to get what they want. They don't focus on the obstacles in front of them but on crossing the finish line, which they see clearly through their mind's eyes. In addition to having a winning attitude, you must be motivated by your needs, your wants, and your passions. Winners not only recognize when such things are absent from their lives, but they also know what it takes to fulfill their goals. That's what winners like Winfrey, Clinton, and Edison did—all in their unique ways.

The average person will not give up something that's important to him or her for an opportunity to gain much more. That's the difference between a winner and someone who settles for mediocrity.

Whatever you believe is what you will put your effort into. If you truly believe you don't need anything more (or don't want anymore) than what you have at this moment, you wouldn't be reading a book about how to become a winner in life.

Why do you want to become a winner?

____

____

47 http://www.businessinsider.com/successful-people-who-were-fired-2015-10

Writing your answers will help you reflect and maintain a wining perspective when things get difficult. Everyone has certain things they want and need. When it comes to someone with a winning mentality, that person knows how to tap into positive thinking and allow it to motivate him or her to push hard until that person succeed. Not only must you know what you want, but you've got to know where you're going. Do you need motivation to get up and start moving toward your dream? Below are some suggestions I hope will do just that—motivate you.

What are you good at, and what do you like to do? Are they the same?

What are your strengths and your weaknesses?

What opportunities await your response for you to respond; what risks are involved in going for those opportunities?

Being realistic about the future, what are your specific goals?

What will it take to accomplish your purpose?

It's never too late to win. If you are a sports fan, you will remember exactly where you were when that spectacular, jaw-dropping play occurred or the exhilaration you felt when your team won the championship game. I'm talking about the kind of plays and games that make you say with incredulity, "Did you just see that?"

My I-can't-believe-that-just-happened moment happened during Monday Night Football, October 6, 2003. It was the Indianapolis Colts versus the Tampa Bay Buccaneers. The Colts were down nineteen points with four minutes to play in the fourth quarter. Any normal person would guess the Tampa Bay Buccaneers had that game in the bag, and rightfully so. After all, they were the defending Super Bowl champion. I imagine that many fans in the stadium left early to beat traffic and some watching the game on TV tuned out before the end to make sure they would arrive to work on time the next morning. But as the saying goes, "It's not over until the fat lady sings." The Indianapolis Colts made a remarkable, record-breaking comeback—the largest comeback in NFL history—winning the game by three points in overtime. No matter how many minutes are on the clock, there's always a chance to win.

Belief, hard work, and perseverance pay off in the end. The Indianapolis Colts could have given up, but they stuck with it and worked hard to put themselves in a winning position. The reward was a miraculous win that went in the history books and is still talked about over a decade later. Hard work, persistence, and, believing you can win will always reward you tremendously.

Winning Thinking

There was a certain boy, about thirteen years old, who was experienced at sheep herding. He demonstrated that there is more than meets the eye when it comes to being a winner.

The boy was about to have the fight of his life against a mighty giant no one could tame. Not only was his opponent much bigger than him, but also, he was much more experienced in battle. The only "fighting" experience the young man had under his belt was killing a lion and a bear to protect his sheep. The giant was a champion fighter, having no defeats on his record. Viewing the competition from a glance, it seems like a no-brainer which of the two was going to come out victorious. One may easily believe the teenage shepherd was pronouncing his own death sentence.

He proved that winning is more mental than physical; it's more of what happens in the mind and what you already know and less about having superior physical strength. Of course, having great skills would help, but how your mind thinks is central to your becoming a winner.

You think so too, right?

No man wanted to fight the giant because the giant's skills were exceptional. They were terrified of him, that is everyone except the teenage shepherd. Bolstered by his faith in God, the lowly shepherd boy stepped up and agreed to meet the giant in battle. He knew his physical stature was no match for the mighty warrior, but he also knew that he wasn't going to rely on bare strength. That is an area of faulty thinking that many people fall into, believing winners look like Mr. Universe or a beauty pageant queen. When in doubt, remember the victory begins in your mind; it starts with how you think.

The boy believed from the start that he could be victorious, not only because of his experience defeating the lion and the bear but because he had someone on his side greater than the giant he was facing. Having a winning attitude will take you a long way. This scrawny teen with the big heart and winning attitude went out to fight the intimidating warrior, carrying only a staff, a sling, and five stones. Whether courageous or foolish, one thing is sure: he believed he could win.

The point of this biblical story about David versus Goliath is that you must be a winner in your mind before you can be a winner in reality. Another way of putting it is you must believe you can do it before you can carry out the task. All it took was one stone in a sling and great faith to take down the giant, who went down like a huge tree being cut by a lumberjack.

Winning thinking is a unique ability we all need to achieve success. Our dreams and goals require it. While everyone may have their own definition of success, which is shaped by their hopes and dreams, those who have attained success credit it to their mindset, which motivates them and, more importantly, gives them the strength to persevere and be consistent doing something every day to achieve their dreams. They don't vacillate between being gung-ho about pursuing their dream one day and questioning whether they have what it takes to realize it the next day.

Desires Required for Becoming a Winner

If you want to win, you must possess the following desires:

- The desire to acquire and possess what you want or need
- The desire to go for it and not just daydream about it
- The desire to do what looks impossible to other people
- The desire to explore and be curious about what would happen if you try
- The desire to act and determine the outcome
- The desire to be highly regarded by others for your winning attitude

Having the mind of a winner consists of being the best you can be and not settling for anything less than what you expect of yourself.

Feed Your Mind

One of country music star Kenny Rogers's most popular songs is "The Gambler." "The Gambler" is a wonderful song about knowing what moves you must make and when to make them in the game of poker. In short, it's a song about timing. Knowing when to make your move is part of the strategy of the game. If you don't know when to make them, you might be in for a miserable time.

Maybe you are not familiar with poker. Maybe it's farming that you know. "There is a time to sow and a time to reap." When it's sowing time, you must make sure that you participate so that when it's time to reap, you will reap whatever you sowed—and what you sow is important. If you neglect to participate in the sowing period, you're going to be left out when the reaping period arrives. So many people have been left out because they didn't realize that you must give to get, bless to be blessed, and so on. As a result, they have not fulfilled their destiny. If you put in the work, you will get the benefit. You must deposit positive thoughts in your mind to get a positive return. Think of it as an investment or saving money toward a major purchase. To improve your financial picture, you may have to change your spending habits, right? Likewise, if you want to change your outlook on life and begin making investments that will yield a winner, you must change the way you think.

Feed your mind only with positive things. If you continue to think and say positive things intentionally, eventually those words will become your automatic response to any given situation. As an exercise, write down positive quotes from Scripture or successful people and meditate on them often.

Put Your Mind into It

I must admit it took me a while figure out the phrase "put your mind into it." I had heard it many times but never paid much attention to it until the day it hit me that I was going to be a single parent to three young boys. You see, after my wife passed away, I was so focused on the void left by her absence, I wasn't motivated to do anything. But then I realized that if I didn't set my mind on changing my situation, my sons would never recover from losing their mother. I would not have been able to provide the best possible life for my boys if I allowed myself to drown in grief forever.

Your current situation—whatever it is—won't change until you make up your mind that you want a different outcome. I had to learn and understand that passion and zeal come from being a go-getter who wins is the result of putting your mind into whatever you have set your heart to do.

You could tell yourself all day, "I can do this," if you really think you can. And if you have the desire to work for it, you will do it. On the other hand, if you tell yourself, "I can't" or "it's just too hard," guess what? You are right—you can't and you won't. Whatever you put your mind into is what you will do, sink or swim.

Let's face it: the road to success is not easy. I don't want to make it seem as though winning is a cinch. No one is going to tap you on the shoulder and magically make you a winner. If your goal is big, you must want it bad enough to overcome the obstacles that will inevitably get in your way. Without a doubt, those obstacles will make you want to give up, but they will also make you stronger. Your desire for reaching your goal has to outweigh the discomfort and pain you may experience on the journey toward it. You must want it so badly that you're willing to sacrifice time and energy to get it. Maybe you have to give up watching your favorite television programs. Maybe you cannot spend as much time hanging with friends. Maybe you have to tighten your budget more than usual, give up cable for a while. Maybe you have to do something even tougher like cut a relationship that's dead weight and only hindering your progress. When you're trying to achieve something major, it will always come with costs. But the reward will far outweigh that. If you want to win, you must be in it for the long haul.

Winners Ignore Obstacles

Once your mind is programmed to automatically think thoughts filled with hope and confidence, it will practically be impossible to detour from the course that leads to success in your life. You are set to go and win! Are you ready to compel your mind to get into winning mode of thinking? Answer these few questions:

> Do you have a hunger and thirst for what you really want or need?
>
> ____
>
> ____
>
> Is it worth your security and stability to push harder, even when you feel you can't push anymore?
>
> ____
>
> ____

If you have identified what you are pursuing as a must-have to survive, are you willing to go the extra mile to get it?

____

____

There is a cost to acquire what you want. How bad do you want the prestige, the success, and the achievement that comes with winning?

____

____

Are you satisfied with where you are right now in your life, or do you feel as though you're missing something?

____

____

Knowledge and understanding are power. How much can you handle?

____

____

Are you sure you're willing to handle all that comes with the privilege of being successful?

____

____

People try to satisfy their wants according to how they feel about what's going on in their lives and the things they find it in. However, the satisfaction of getting what you want can be risky depending on how hard it is to acquire it. A true winner will usually go for it despite the risks.

At this point, I want you to take a moment and meditate on the things you really want out of your life, and decide whether those things are worth the effort and risk to give it your all to get them. Write your answers below or in your journal so that you can always refer to them and mark the date they come to fruition in your life.

Once you feel that you've had enough time to think and have written down all that you want from life, turn to the next chapter.

Chapter Five: Ignite Your Desire

The will to win, the desire to succeed, the urge to reach your full potential... these are the keys that will unlock the door to personal excellence.

- Confucius

Do you know what the number one New Year's resolution is? Yep, you guessed it: losing weight or exercising more. Of the 41 percent of Americans who typically make New Year's resolutions, over 20 percent of them resolve to get in shape.[48] Twelve percent desire to improve their lives in some way and 8.5 percent want to make smarter money choices. The list goes on. But if I were to survey those same people who set out to shed a few pounds or get out of debt, how many of them do you think reached their goal?

With every good intention, including announcing their resolutions to the world on social media—with inspiring images to boot—most people simply won't reach their goal. They won't even come close. According to Statisticbrain.com, less than ten percent of all people who make New Year's resolutions keep them. So, are you a part of the nine percent who "feel" they are successful at achieving what they set out to do or the ninety percent who fall by the wayside? If I were a betting person, I would go with the odds and say you're a part

---

[48] http://www.statisticbrain.com/new-years-resolution-statistics/

of the ninety percent, and if you are, the question is why—or better yet, how bad did you want it in the first place?

So, how bad do you want it? How much to do you want to grow or become a better version of yourself (by the way, over 44 percent of New Year's resolution are based on self-improvement)[49]. Have you ever wanted something so bad you would do anything to get it? That's what I want to talk to you about in this chapter: getting out of the park position and developing the drive toward fulfilling your desires.

At one time or another, we all desire something or someone. A career opportunity. A love interest. Two scoops of our favorite flavor of ice cream. And yes, often we want a beach-ready body while eating the ice cream. But the journey toward winning doesn't lead down an easy road.

Whether or not we obtain the thing we desire boils down to doing the right thing at the right time (our actions), which is fueled by our mindset (our thoughts). There's a well-known saying, you are what you eat. (If you consume two scoops of ice cream nearly every day, forget the beach body.) Likewise, you are also what you think. Thoughts such as "I don't know if I have what it takes" will get you nowhere near attaining the success you dream about.

Our longing for something must be fed before it can be manifested. We must believe we can achieve whatever we set our minds to do and then act on that desire to fulfill it. As Statisticbrain.com demonstrates in its tally of those who make and keep their New Year's resolutions, only a few people can find the way to make it work out the way they would like. It's not because they are lucky or have access to resources others

---

[49] http://www.statisticbrain.com/new-years-resolution-statistics/

don't, although the latter may be true. However, they do have access to one resource we all have: the mind. The way you think can move your desire forward or backward. If your thoughts are generally positive and you possess a can-do attitude, even when you experience setbacks (which are part of growing) you will likely fulfill your desires (and just so I am clear, I am speaking of your desire to grow, to build, to excel, to prosper). But if your thinking stinks, your desires will be nothing more than a pipe dream. Well, guess what? It happens to the best of us. That inability or unwillingness to move or the terrible habit of procrastinating, always promising to start tomorrow, is a very human trait. Despite all the good intentions we have in our hearts, we just don't do it. So, it that's your struggle, how do you push past that and make your desires reality?

Manifested Desires

Psychologist **Abraham Maslow** believed that "once people were fed, they would be off in search of success or some other form of interpersonal satisfaction." When we talk about being fed, our fuel could come from information we learn or just intrinsic knowledge. More often than not, go-getters and procrastinators want the same thing, but what separates one from the other? How does the one group succeed, but the other does not?

I will tell you.

The difference comes in how well they are satisfied. Whether you consume natural food or information, you must eat until you are satisfied. If you are not satisfied, something is missing. Let's say you don't eat enough natural food during the day. At one point, you will begin to feel weak, or your stomach will indicate with an empty feeling and a growl that it's not satisfied. In any case, you have to consume more. And most likely you will. So why not approach your goals and dreams the same way? Keep feeding them. By the way, you are not supposed to get full when it comes to learning and growing. For example, let's say you love dogs and want to start a pet grooming business, but you don't know the first thing about pet grooming, let alone starting a business. Now that's a daunting goal to accomplish, and it would appear you have a few high hurdles to jump. But you can realize that goal, especially if you depend on God because nothing is impossible for Him, right? So, the first order of business is to believe you can do it. The next thing you want to do is learn how to groom a dog. So, you look for schools or training programs that will teach you how. If you find one and discover you don't have money for the fee, don't say, "I can't afford the class." Say instead, "I will save the money I need for the class." Once you have the money, you take the training, complete the training, and get a job at a pet store or with a dog grooming service to put what you've learned to work and begin learning how such a business works. But you don't allow yourself to get super comfortable. You have to watch out for that on your journey toward fulfilling a big dream because it's easy to get comfortable in one situation along the way and forget about the ultimate destination. All while you're working and honing your skills, you are still saving money, researching online and via interviews and books how to build and run a dog grooming business, and maybe even taking a general business course. Before you realize it, the day arrives when you open your pet grooming business. But you don't stop there. You continue to feed that desire by always seeking ways to grow as a groomer and a business owner, staying abreast of the latest developments in your field and only resting if and when you reach a point when it's time to sell your business or retire.

There may be steps to starting a dog grooming business I didn't mention. But the point I'm trying to make is that some people give up too soon or too easily before the manifestation of their dream takes place. That is what separates a winner from a loser. For instance, let's say two writers with two different manuscripts query an editor or book publisher about publishing their work. They both receive rejection letters. The writer with a defeated mindset will likely internalize the rejection as a sign he isn't good enough and will let his dream die right there. He may end up stewing for a while before he occasionally revisits his dream or the idea of fulfilling it, never getting any further than his imagination. But the writer with a winning mindset may view the rejection as poor taste on the editor's part or simply not a good fit for his book and move on to querying the next publisher and the next until he gets the answer he's looking for. *Zen and the Art of Motorcycle Maintenance* was rejected 121 times before it became a bestselling book read by millions.[50] Because Author Robert Pirsig never gave up his desire to publish his work, millions of readers have gained invaluable insight into the meaning of their lives

The biggest difference between winners and losers is not talent or ability, but how they respond to setbacks or failure, which is an inevitable part of the growth process.

Here are some traits winners exhibit on their way to accomplishing their goals:

---

[50] http://entertainment.howstuffworks.com/arts/literature/14-best-selling-books-repeatedly-rejected-by-publishers8.htm

- Winners have an unbreakable desire to acquire knowledge and put what they've learned into action.
- Winners have a passion that compels them to connect and associate with influential people.
- Winners have the desire to influence and motivate others.
- Winners want to help others get to the next level.

Of course, you must understand that you can have all the desire in the world to accomplish your goal, but it means nothing until you get started. At this point, I want you to write down the ten things you most desire. The objective in recording your desires on paper is to have a written record you can review and use as inspiration for making a move toward fulfilling them.

1____

2____

3____

4____

5____

6____

7____

8____

9____

10____

Finished? Here is where you will begin to take action. Create and put in place a fool-proof plan that will not fade away within the next couple of weeks like a New Year's resolution. Do whatever it takes to schedule and organize your life so that you have no interruptions during your calls to action. In other words, when you make the plan an important part of your regular routine, everything begins to fall into place.

Fulfilling Your Desires

Going for "it"—or fulfilling your deepest desires—is risky, depending on how hard you're willing to work to get what you want. Some people are only ready to work according to how they feel at a particular moment. Some people may just want power while others want prestige. Nevertheless, winners will usually put their all into reaching milestones and reaching their goal regardless of how they feel because they remain focused on the greater picture. If someone has a goal to lose ten pounds in thirty days, with a plan to run five miles every day for six days a week, they don't wake up on day one of the journey and decide not to go to the gym or hit the pavement because they're too tired or it's chilly outside. Sure, she's still tired, and she doesn't like the cold, but she prioritizes her weight-loss goal. Besides, once she arrives at the gym, the sleepiness has worn off. Her body has warmed up after several minutes into her run, and she no longer feels the chill of the cold air.

Remember that the race toward the finish line is not a sprint but a marathon. It's not fast food but a gourmet meal that takes time to prepare. Reaching your goal—whatever it may be—will take time if you're willing to put in the work to become a true winner.

Many of us watched the Olympic Games and are fascinated by the abilities of Olympic athletes. Although many of us will never come close to running an Olympic race, we all are in this race called life, and the ultimate goal is to win at it. So, we must approach it the same way an Olympic athlete trains four years for one moment. Sometimes life isn't fair, is it? It seems to dole out strength, talent, and abilities unevenly: a few appear to have it all, while many of us have to work hard to get the little we have. This truth reminds me of a Scripture from the Bible: "The race is not to the swift, nor the battle to the strong" (Ecclesiastes 9:11). If you can conquer or prevail over the obstacles and challenges you will inevitably face and endure to the end, you will become a winner. Remember these words from filmmaker Woody Allen, "Seventy percent of success in life is showing up."[51]

---

[51] https://www.brainyquote.com/quotes/quotes/w/woodyallen105320.html

Getting Started

Start small just to get you going. Don't try to conquer the world in one day. As the saying goes, "Rome wasn't built in a day." Be realistic and establish a goal that is readily achievable to start. Commit yourself to doing it and not just trying to do it; not doing it isn't an option. Sometimes we make an effort, but within no time we fall back into our old habits. Don't let anything stop you from making your desires come true. When you commit to doing it, hold yourself accountable. If you have to involve someone else to help you monitor your progress and hold you responsible, go ahead and do it. That person will make sure you think twice about ditching your action plan. You must be able to keep yourself motivated. It may require replacing the time you normally spend watching television with reading a personal development book, taking a webinar, or doing research. Find other things to push you. You may have to find a group of friends who have similar goals or who understand what you are trying to do. Those types of friends won't get upset when you have to occasionally skip a time of socializing because they know or respect the sacrifices you need to make to reach your goal. Once you begin to see progress and others around you begin to comment on that progress, telling you how great you're doing, you will feel good about your decision to pursue your dream.

This final piece of advice is essential. You will be tempted at times to give up and quit. A setback, a closed door, or rejection will discourage you and may make you want to wave the white flag of surrender. Don't give up! Keep going no matter what you encounter or what obstacles you face. Get up, shake off the hit to your confidence, stop throwing big pity parties, and keep moving forward. I promise you this: if you don't quit, you'll arrive at your destination and witness your dream come true.

You are a winner.

Chapter 6: From Dreamer to Doer

"A dream doesn't become reality through magic; it takes sweat, determination, and hard work."

~Colin Powell

One of the worst things we can do is compare ourselves to others and conclude we're not as good or talent or fortunate, especially when we haven't taken one step toward fulfilling our dreams. It's easy to fall prey to negative emotions like envy and depression and find ourselves asking God, "What about me?" when we're scrolling through our Facebook news feed and being bombarded by all the success of our "Friends," those we know "for real" and those we're still trying to figure out how we know at all. The excitement of a new romance, the celebration of a wedding anniversary, the announcement of a promotion, the bragging of a child going off to college—all these happy, winning moments in the lives of our "Friends" make those of us who don't have a new relationship, children, or a promotion to boast about feel some type of way. We may like the post and even post a congratulatory comment. "I'm so happy for you!" While on the one hand, we're genuinely happy for our friends, on the other hand we compare our lives to our friends and wonder why they have been blessed in areas we haven't.

Did you know that Facebook overload can make one jealous and depressed, particularly if it becomes a measure by which one determines his or her accomplishments or worth?[52] When we compare ourselves to others, no matter what fuels the comparison, there are a couple of things we can't see.

First, we have no idea how hard our "Friends" worked to experience the success they report on their social media pages (although these days, people freely share their trials as much as they do their triumphs). Second, we don't consider that God has a unique plan for each of us. What God has for your "Friends" is for them, and what He has for you is for you.

So when you find yourself wondering where you are in life and when it will be your turn to share your winning moments with "Friends," answer this question: if you have big dreams for your future, are you willing to do whatever it takes to make them happen? Are you going to remain a dreamer only, which is easy and comfortable to do; or are you going to be a doer, which requires sacrifice, hard work, and persistence? You must decide which you are and know that only one of those choices leads to real success and satisfaction.

Brian Tracy, an entrepreneur and motivational speaker who helps individuals and organizations meet their personal and business goals once said, "All successful people men and women are big dreamers. They imagine what their future could be, ideal in every respect, and then they work every day toward their distant vision, that goal or purpose." [53] Just because you want something, even if you pray for it, doesn't mean you'll automatically receive it without an effort

---

[52] https://www.forbes.com/sites/alicegwalton/2013/01/22/jealous-of-your-facebook-friends-why-social-media-makes-us-bitter/#5247f90635cc

[53] https://www.brainyquote.com/quotes/quotes/b/briantracy163247.html

on your part. To borrow from an unsourced quote, "No one is going to hand success to you; you have to go out and get it yourself."[54]

I remember when my desire to write inspirational books was just that, a desire. As time passed, and I remained stuck in that place of wanting to become an author but making no effort to pick up my pen and write, my dream began to look as though it would never come true. Slowly, I began to move on it when I started listening to motivational speakers and life coaches like Les Brown and Tony Robins. I also followed ministers like Bishop T.D. Jakes and Creflo Dollar. Their messages motivated me to begin equipping myself with the knowledge I needed to learn how to write books. I started reading books on the subject—a whole lot of them. Then one day I realized that if I didn't try and *just do it,* writing would always be just a dream. Over preparing can be a form of procrastination as well. Guess what happened? I finally did it. I started writing and never looked back. And today, I have published over ten books, including this one in your hands. In the words of Christ, "Everything is possible for one who believes."[55]

Making Your Dreams Come True Starts with Helping Others

Lailah Gifty Akita said, "Never believe those who say you can't. You can make it in life. Believe in your dreams. You

[54] http://www.keepinspiring.me/famous-quotes-about-success/
[55] Mark 9:23, NIV

can make all your dreams come true."[56] Everyone has a dream or passion, and we are empowered by God's grace to walk it out in this life. Most people hope to one day look over their lives and declare they are living well. One of the marks of success is living well, and it should be. However, to make your dreams a reality requires your giving as much as you receive. It involves encouraging and guiding others. As Jesus Himself teaches us, it's always better to give than to receive.[57] If you take your eyes off you and place them on someone else, you will be surprised how quickly your dream begins to unfold. Have you ever noticed how some successful people strive to bring out the best in others by setting a good example? Motivational speaker and life coach Mel Robbins is one such person. Here's the thing: she wasn't always a motivational speaker and life coach. In a recent Creative Live class, she admitted to her audience of having once hopped from one career to the next, from one business venture to the next, until she finally found her stride. Today she's doing what she's passionate about: helping others overcome the very thing that had dogged her for years, which was self-doubt, to become their best selves and fulfill their dreams.[58]

Successful people like Robbins reach out to others and help them climb the ladder of success. They trust people, believe in them, and have faith in them. They genuinely care about people and their outcomes. And by doing so, they plant the seeds of success in their own lives. They don't worry about getting something in return (unfortunately, some people

---

[56] https://www.goodreads.com/quotes/6588738-never-believe-those-who-says-you-can-t-you-can-you

[57] Acts 20:35

[58] Mel Robbins, "How to Break the Habit of Self-Doubt and Build Real Confidence," aired on CreativeLive.com, August 30, 2017

only give with the motive of receiving). Their primary concern is planting seeds of hope and encouragement. The apostle Paul said to the Corinthians, "I planted the seed in your hearts, and Apollos watered it, but it was God who made it grow. It's not important who does the planting, or who does the watering. What's important is that God makes the seed grow. The one who plants and the one who waters work together with the same purpose. And both will be rewarded for their own hard work."[59]

Every Sunday, my pastor ends our worship service by reminding the congregation to "love somebody, love everybody." That's what winning is truly about. More than acquiring wealth, gaining prestige and fame, or being promoted, you win when you show compassion toward others and when you desire to see people live fruitful and satisfying lives. I believe what my pastor means by that is if you show love, love will return to you. Likewise, when you give, you will receive. When you share—resources, knowledge, time—others will share with you. When you help people, people will go out of their way to help you. Bottom line: if you want to be successful in life, help someone. Then watch what happens next.

Diversity Creates Winning

Hillary Clinton made history when in the summer of 2016 she became the first woman to be named the nominee for the presidency of the United States by a major political party. Her campaign slogan was "We are Stronger Together," which

---

[59] 1 Corinthians 3:6-8, NLT

echoes my sentiment that winning is not a solo act. Despite what some people would like to believe, successful people got to where they are by pulling themselves up by their own bootstraps. Working with and helping others is the foundation of acquiring success.

If I can borrow Clinton's slogan for a moment, what does it really mean to be stronger together? Think of a 1000-piece puzzle. Unlinked, those pieces serve no purpose. When the top is removed from the box, they are nothing more than a pile of colorful tiles with potential. But when they come together, linked by a patient and persistent hand willing to sort through the pieces for as long as it takes to figure out how they connect, they form the beautiful photo on the top of the box—the finished product. Now think of those pieces as people.

When people from various backgrounds and abilities come together—despite their differences and even because of their differences—they make one strong body, a requisite for succeeding collectively and individually. When separated and on their own; however, those pieces are extremely weak. When a person decides to pursue a goal alone in his or her own way—without advice—on his or her own, ignoring the fact no one excels without some help along the way, he will plateau or stall in his growth until he realizes he's stronger when he connects with others. Here's what Clinton said about the meaning of her campaign slogan during an interview with journalist Chuck Todd:

> Look, we are stronger together. We are stronger together, in facing our internal challenges and our external ones. We are stronger together if we work to improve the economy. And that's going to mean trying to get the Republicans to do what will help produce more jobs, like we saw in the 1990s. We are stronger together when we have a

bipartisan, even nonpartisan foreign policy that protects our country. And that provides a kind of steady, strong, smart leadership that the rest of the world expects from us. And I know that … slogans come and go, and all the rest of it. But when I look at where we are in our country together, we need to unify the country. We are stronger together when we act on a set of plans and priorities that will redound to the benefit of the American people.[60]

Seventeenth-century English author John Donne put it this way, "No man is an island. No one is self-sufficient; everyone relies on each other." Whether you believe it's just a coincidence or an unfortunate situation, every living soul lives under the same sky and walks the same surface. We interact in more ways than we realize. Humans are created in such a way that we cannot exist without relying on each other. Strength, power, and greatness come from diversity. And it takes a special ability to use diversity—in race, gender, age, community, education, personality type—to cultivate a oneness to achieve a goal.

As you strive to get on a winning track in life, don't do so blindly. Don't approach goal setting and attaining success with a selfish view. Think long-term and include others in your plan, which will yield an even greater return on your investment of time, resources, and energy. "Give, and you shall receive, your gift will return to you in full—pressed down, shaken together to make room for more, running over,

[60] https://www.nbcnews.com/meet-the-press/meet-press-may-22-2016-n578291

and poured into your lap. The amount you give will determine the amount you get back."[61]

During the semi-final of the 5,000-meter heat of track and field at the Summer Olympics in Rio, the unthinkable happened to American runner Abbey Agostino.[62] In the middle of the heat, she bumped into her competitor Nikki Hamblin of New Zealand, who had slowed down to keep from colliding with another runner, and they both fell to the track. D'Agostino quickly got back up but noticed Hamblin writhing in pain on the ground. Instead of trying to catch up with the rest of the pack, she reached down to help her fellow runner get to her feet. But D'Agostino realized at that moment that her ankle was severely sprained, and she couldn't continue running but encouraged Hamblin to keep running and cross the finish line. Although Hamblin was her competitor, in that devastating moment, D'Agostino put someone else's needs ahead of her own. After the race, Hamblin praised her rival for demonstrating the true Olympic spirit by encouraging her to finish the race when D'Agostino herself could not.

Earlier, when I talked about the importance of winning, I stressed how the world around us only remembers the person or team who ends up in first place. But what D'Agostino demonstrated that day is that winning isn't always about finishing first or winning a medal. It's about finishing, period. It's about not giving up. It's about displaying sportsmanship, empathy, and charity. It's about love for our fellow man or woman. You don't always have to come in first place to be a winner.

---

[61] Luke 6:38, NLT

[62] http://www.latimes.com/sports/olympics/la-sp-oly-rio-2016-runners-abbey-d-agostino-nikki-hamblin-1471369602-htmlstory.html

Real winners are role models. They're not interested in having or forcing their way but in finding the best way. They work hard, and they work together. They are successful because of their application, resoluteness, and perseverance. Yes, winners are dreamers, but they are also doers; they don't allow their dreams to lie dormant, suppressed by fear, doubt, procrastination, what if*s*, and if only*s*. They are self-starters with open minds who create plans and set them in motion. They pursue personal goals with tenacity while at the same time helping others reach higher levels of performance.

Are you ready to kick-start the process for making your dreams come true? Are you ready to move from just dreaming to doing? Let's look at some practices you can incorporate into your life daily that will strengthen your resolve to get up and start moving toward your dream, and more important to finish what you start.

Prayer and Faith

While this book is not written strictly to Christians, I would be negligent not to mention the role your relationship with God places in fulfilling your dreams. If God is not in the equation, any success you gain is empty. And the best way to keep God in front and center of your goals is to know Him and communicate with Him regularly through prayer.

Carve out time to pray and seek God's guidance, and commit to it; consider it a meeting with your heavenly manager, as God is the CEO of your life. You can even write down your talking points as you would with a human boss. Listen to what God has to say about each area you pray about, and wait for His direction. And when you seek God in prayer, don't do all the talking. Listen to His voice so that you know exactly how to pursue your dream. I believe Priscilla Shirer says it best: "Creating time, space, and opportunity to hear God is paramount for those of us who desire to sense His Spirit's conviction, to receive His detailed guidance, and to discern His intimate leading."[63]

And believe Him when He shows you things about your future, even when something He's showing you seems impossible or unlikely or is taking longer than you would like to manifest. That's where your faith comes in. Write this definition of faith on a card and place it somewhere you can see and recite it every day: "The fundamental fact of existence is that this trust in God, this faith, is the firm foundation under everything that makes life worth living. It's our handle on what we can't see."[64]

Most people whose dreams come true have a vision that's anchored by faith (what they believe and in whom they believe) and prayer (daily communication with whom they believe and the one who guides them). More so than fulfilling a dream, they are seeking their purpose to make sure it aligns with God's will for their lives. To get more in-depth on this subject, see my book *Pursuing Your Purpose: How to Discover God's Revelation for Your Life.*

Having faith is critical to your success. A lack of faith cost many of the Israelites who escaped slavery in Egypt their dream of reaching the Promised Land. They died in the desert. And despite his great belief in God, it cost Moses being able to

---

[63] Shirer, Priscilla. *Discerning the Voice of God: How to Recognize When God Is Speaking*. (Chicago: Moody Publishers, 2007, 2012), p. 18.
[64] Hebrews 11:1-2, The Message Bible

lead them in. One mistake can be costly, but it can also be a set-up of victory for someone else.

Meditation

So, you may be thinking, isn't prayer meditation? It's not. While prayer is about communicating your need and getting direction, meditation is about concentrating on those instructions. It's about honing in on that definition of faith I suggested you write down and recite daily, and burying its meaning deep within you so that eventually you don't have to work hard to conjure up belief at the moment a challenge arises because it's in you already. Meditation is the way we master our faith and change our thoughts for good. One of the earliest examples we can find meditation playing a significant role in someone fulfilling their destiny is in the life of Joshua, a protégé of Moses. Joshua's faith in God led to a big appointment. I want to elaborate on the story I ended the last section with.

God hand-picked Moses, Joshua's predecessor, to lead the children of Israel out of Egypt, where they had been slaves for centuries. Moses was hesitant about his role at first, thinking he didn't have what it took to confront Pharaoh and demand the freedom of God's people, but he eventually grew into the role through prayer and faith! God equipped Moses with everything he needed to confront Pharaoh, and after a lot of going back and forth and a series of plagues that led up to a devastating wave of death that wiped out the firstborn of every Egyptian, including the Pharaoh's son, Moses was successful in the first leg of his assignment. He led Israel out of Egypt, out of bondage, and not without a shortage of high drama.

There was a chase, a parting of the Red Sea, a conquering of the enemy, and a safe arrival to freedom across the bottom of a dry seabed. Moses led millions of people out of slavery into freedom. But as it is with fickle humanity, those people soon began to complain about being in the desert and wondering whether they were better off where they were. That's exactly how we get when we lose sight of what God has declared to us about our dreams our future and turn to reason rather than faith. Moses was supposed to lead those people to a designated place that God directed him to go, a land of milk and honey. However, the constant complaining of the people eventually caught Moses' last nerve. In a moment of frustration, He disobeyed God's direction. As a result of not following God's instruction to the letter, he fell short of being able to lead the people into the Promised Land.

That's where Joshua comes into play.

Joshua was about to take over a great ministry from Moses. His assignment was to pick up where Moses left off and lead the Israelites who did not die in the desert into Canaan, the land of milk and honey.

Joshua was about to embark on something new and challenging in his life. Although he was a soldier, leading Israel into already occupied territory was much more responsibility than he had ever had before. He was no longer taking orders from another man. He now had to give them, and him to make decisions that could make or break the people he was leading. Joshua had no choice but to walk closer to God if he intended to fulfill that assignment. And one of the things he had to learn was how to meditate on God's directives and principles for living. " This set of instructions is not to cease being a part of your conversations. Meditate on it day and night, so that you may be careful to carry out everything that's written in it, for then you'll prosper and succeed."[65]

God told Joshua to meditate on the instructions he received for guiding the group. Meditation is another word for thinking. It's deep thinking. Whatever you keep in your mind constantly will eventually show up in your actions. That's why winners are recognized as productive people; they take time to develop the strategy they need to implement to succeed or reach their goals. They then meditate on it day and night to gain a clear understanding of what they must do to succeed. Successful people manage their minds as efficiently as they manage their business. God told Joshua if he kept thinking about the instructions He gave Him and applied them that he would succeed and prosper.

Have you ever heard the saying, "Watch your thoughts; they become words. Watch your words; they become actions. Watch your actions; they become habits. Watch your habits; they become character. Watch your character; it becomes your DESTINY"? I believe that's exactly what God was telling Joshua as it related to Joshua's assignment. Whatever you keep forefront in your mind constantly will shape your final destination.

If meditation is new for you or you're not sure how to approach it, there are things you can do the following things to help you get in the right frame of mind:

Read: Reading is a major part of success, but it's not just what you read but what you comprehend that makes the difference. Remember, when Joshua was given his marching orders, he was told to meditate on the

[65] Joshua 1:8 (ISV)

instructions God had given Moses, which was the book of the Law of Moses.

To be a winner, read as much as you can; read something every day: articles, books, blogs, and so on. Always look for new sources of wisdom, knowledge, and inspiration to enrich your spirit and give you new insights about your plan.

Relax: Winners work hard and long, but winners also know the importance of balance and rest. Jesus—the greatest winner in history—modeled the need for relaxation. It helps us hear more clearly. If you're stressed out or worn out all the time, you'll find it difficult to meditate on God's instructions to you, let alone follow them. It will never profit you to stretch yourself thin and to the point of burnout. If you desire to be a winner, you must recognize that relaxing is just as productive as working. That's why winners find the time to relax and meditate.

Also take time to exercise, eat and drink in moderation, and maintain a sense of humor. Don't take yourself so seriously; laugh at yourself now and then. And if that's hard to do, go see a comedian. The point I'm trying to make is add some humor to your life.

Relax and think thoughts that release peace, quiet, and tranquility into your spirit. Find someplace where you can hear the wind blowing in the trees or watch the rolling waves of the ocean (if you live in a coastal area). Watch the sunset sometimes. In other words, take time to feel the power of nature. "Looking at beauty in the world is the first step of purifying the mind."[66]

The objective is to have a level head. Living with the stress of everyday life can cause you to lose sight and control of your purpose. But meditation is one of the ways to get the best out of thinking positively a topic we'll delve into more deeply in chapter eleven; however, I want to touch on it a bit now.

Thinking

Whatever you think about continually will come likely happen. Trust me. That's why it's so important that you keep your mind on the things you are trying to accomplish. Your thoughts are part of your mind's eye, what you see in your head and what you envision. If you see yourself flopping on a project because you feel overwhelmed by the challenge, you likely will flop. So, don't envision failure in anything. Successful minded people set no limits to their thoughts. They use their imaginations to create the outcomes they want to see, knowing that someday and somehow those dreams will come true.

It's been said that "humans are thinking animals—any thinking person would approve." However, thinking is not the problem; the problem lies between the thinking and the winning. In today's microwave-paced style of living, the

---

[66] Quote by Amit Ray, https://www.goodreads.com/quotes/357605-looking-at-beauty-in-the-world-is-the-first-step

ability to wait for the manifestation of a thought is limited. People want it now.

Making Sound Decisions

Whatever direction you take will be the result of the decision you make. If you make wise decisions, you'll be headed in the right direction. Likewise, if you make a poor decision, you'll be off course: lost. This is where I urge you to carefully take your time to think through your decisions before you finalize them, especially when the lives of others or money is involved. It's always better to take your time and not make a rash decision because one decision will change the course of your life. Remember how Moses' one decision cost him being able to lead the children of Israel into the Promised Land? His decision: to strike the rock instead of only speaking to it as God had commanded Him. What may seem like a small thing can have a major consequence. So, take your time to ensure the decisions you're making are smart ones.

Making the correct decision is your goal because that's how you'll get the results you desire. Here are some best practices to consider implementing in your decision making to ensure you always make the right choices:

> **Never make a decision under pressure**. Be sure you have a clear and defined understanding of what you are about to do or say. When you take a moment to relax and meditate, you will see the bigger picture. In other words, think before you act, for your decision could determine whether you win or lose.

Never make a decision when you are in pain or in the heat of the moment. For example, don't make decisions immediately following a disagreement with your spouse, a family feud, or an argument with a friend. When decisions are made out of frustration and anger, they tend to be the wrong ones because emotion clouds them. As a result, those decisions can end up causing more harm than good—and no one wins when that happens. Also, don't make major decisions immediately following significant emotional turmoil in your life, such as the death of a loved one.

Never decide to get revenge. Some people may not believe this, but good always prevails over evil. And when it does, you want to be on the side of good because you will reap what you sow. So, make it your goal always to take the high road in a situation where you're in conflict with someone, or you feel you've been wronged. In the words of the good book, "Never pay back evil with more evil. Do things in such a way that everyone can see you are honorable. Do all that you can to live in peace with everyone. Dear friends, never take revenge. Leave that to the righteous anger of God."[67] In other words, God's got your back.

When making a decision, always think ahead. Think about what's going to occur down the road, months and years after you've made that decision. Think for tomorrow and not just for today. If you follow these simple steps, you will make good decisions and end up a winner in every aspect of your life.

---

[67] Romans 12:17-19a, NLT

Persistence Pays

Calvin Coolidge, the thirtieth president of the United States, said nothing could take the place of persistence. [68] Not talents. Believe me, the world is full of unsuccessful people with talent, and I'm sure you know some of them. Not even an excellent education. The world is also full of well-educated derelicts. Talent, education, and even genius amount to very little without persistence. But persistence and determination alone will take you to the ends of the world and back. Mastering a "don't quit" attitude alone will always drive you to your expected end and beyond.

Winners know that if a dream is worth having, it's worth the effort of pursuit. They know it's worth the sacrifice, the sweat, and the tears that accompany the journey toward success. With their eyes on the prize, they persist. Have you ever been in line at a store behind a customer who insisted on getting a certain price on an item? She waited patiently while the cashier called for a price check, even if it meant further delaying an already long line. She doesn't care that it's Saturday morning and the store is packed and that people behind her may be running behind to their next appointment. She is going to wait for as long as it takes for the cashier to come up with the price she's willing to pay for that item.

If you want to be a winner, you must see work as a blessing and not a curse. After all, the end goal of that work—your dream—is not going to be handed to you on a silver platter; you have work hard to get it. If you could peek into

[68] http://www.quotationspage.com/quote/2771.html

the mind of a successful person, you will see their work ethic making a significant contribution to their progress. Work isn't something to do just because they have to do it. Keep in mind that you must know when and where to put in the work, so you can eventually live and enjoy your life.

Winners know any level of growth depends on activity, the work they put in. They realize that there is no development, physically or intellectually, without effort. And the effort must be persistent. I once heard someone say, "Work eliminates fear, worry, loneliness, and discouragement and is also the key to success." So, if you desire to be successful, you must work at it with persistence.

Before we move on to the next chapter, I want to stress there is no time limit for attaining success in anything you set out to do. Deciding to get up and do something, especially after being stymied by fear and doubt, is a winning move in and of itself. Also, keep in mind that the process and timetable for each person is different. Ultimately, you are on God's time. So, again, the most important thing is taking action; it's moving forward and making sure all of your decisions and actions are deliberately tied to your dream.

Chapter 7: Your Attitude Determines Altitude

"The greatest discovery of all time is that a person can change his future by merely changing his attitude."

~ Oprah Winfrey

As we discussed in the previous chapter, when it comes to winning, talent, skill, a stable personality, and a good work ethic can take you far, but attitude is everything.

In an article published in *Entrepreneur* magazine several years ago, author Bob Reiss described twelve "attitudes" for being successful in business, writing this: "The key to beating the competition and achieving success is mental, reflected in one's attitude, totally controlled by the individual and requires no cash. This holds true in most human endeavors besides business—in sports, the arts and politics."[69]

Reiss was writing directly to small-business owners, but his advice applies to anyone who wants to be successful in any area. If you're planning to get married or you're already married, you want a successful marriage, right? Then make sure you have a good attitude about everything. If you work

---

[69] https://www.entrepreneur.com/article/204504

for a company where the competition for moving up is stiff, how will you handle the challenges that may get in your way as you try to climb the ladder of corporate success? With the right attitude of course.

So, what is the right approach?

Attitude Defined

An attitude is a settled way of thinking about someone or something, one that is often reflected in a person's behavior, body posture, or tone of voice. Thus, your attitude is a direct reflection of what you think and how you feel about a situation. It is both mental and emotional.

Your attitude can cause you to be either happy or miserable. In most cases, it's not just the place or the condition that impacts your mood but how you respond to what's happening, which is more evident in your posture than your words. Have you ever had a tense conversation with someone that ended on a sour but peaceable note, with the person saying she was fine but the wrinkles in her brow and the stern purse of her lips told you otherwise? If you walked away wondering if she was telling the truth, you would've been right to question her. I think John Maxwell says it best, "People may hear your words, but they feel your attitude."[70]

The attitude of a winner will stand out in a crowded room. Having a winning attitude shows the confidence you have in yourself about what you're trying to accomplish. And it reveals who you are inside. To get on the winning track in life,

[70] https://www.brainyquote.com/quotes/quotes/j/johncmaxw451128.html

it's critical we adopt a positive attitude overall. I want to break down what that positive attitude should look like.

Be Happy

As long as you keep your mind full of rich thoughts, your heart full of positive emotions, and your body doing productive things, you will never be unhappy. Or perhaps a better way to say it is that you will always have peace of mind because the lesson we all must learn is how to be content no matter where we find ourselves along life's journey.

You will have disappointments in life to be sure. For instance, if you lose someone you love to illness or a tragic accident, no one expects you to be happy about it. The challenge is to always be at peace with ourselves and our situations, including the things we can and cannot control, such as the death of a loved one. Maybe it's a situation where you applied for a new job but didn't get hired despite having a couple of interviews. Are you disappointed? More than likely, especially if it was a position you wanted. But are you at peace? Of course, because you've been working hard, you know that if you didn't get the job it wasn't because you're not good enough for it or even that you interviewed poorly. You are content with the employer's decision to hire someone else because you have faith that if you didn't get that job, there's a better one on the horizon. Ideally, that is how maintaining "happiness" at all times looks. It is how we choose to respond to every situation, good and bad, that enables us always to be happy. The kind of happiness I am referring to is contentment or satisfaction, and it's also a choice we condition ourselves to make until over time it becomes an automatic response.

The mind is the seat of perception, self-consciousness, thinking, belief, memory, hope, desire, will, judgment, analysis, evaluation, and reason. To accomplish success requires that you change your mind—get away from selfish and negative thinking, which is part of human nature. To respond negatively to a negative situation is much more natural than responding positively, I get that. But it's possible to change that automatic response. Let's consider some basic definitions to get a clearer picture of the important role our minds play in dictating our outcomes:

Mind—the seat of thought and memory—the center of consciousness that generates thoughts, feelings, ideas, and perceptions, as well as stores knowledge and memories.

Thinking capacity—the ability to think, understand, and reason.

Desire—the desire or intention to act or behave in a particular way.

Way of thinking—an opinion or personal way of thinking, as in "I have changed my

mind about going with you."

If you examine your life, you will find that some areas need more improvement than others. Some are strong, some are weak, and some just need fine-tuning. The adjustments you make to your mindset will reveal some things (or attitudes) in your life that you did not realize were there.

When you examine your life, you identify what you can and cannot do, what you want to improve in and what you want to eliminate. You may cringe as you revisit your mistakes and realize your need or desire for a second chance (or thank God for already giving you one).

Martha Washington, the inaugural First Lady of our nation, once said, "I am determined to be cheerful and happy in whatever situation I may find myself. For I have learned that the greater part of our misery or unhappiness is determined not by our circumstance but by our disposition."[71] The apostle Paul said it this way:

I'm glad in God, far happier than you would ever guess—happy that you're again showing such strong concern for me. Not that you ever quit praying and thinking about me. You just had no chance to show it. Actually, I don't have a sense of needing anything personally. I've learned by now to be quite content whatever my circumstances. I'm just as happy with little as with much, with much as with little. I've found the recipe for being happy whether full or hungry, hands full or hands empty. Whatever I have, wherever I am, I can make it through anything in the One who makes me who I am.[72]

Happiness is a state of mind, having the attitude that you have hope in good times and trying times and look forward to the things to come. Happy people are pleased with what they can achieve and don't get easily bent out of shape when they get caught in life's storms. At the same time, they are motivated to do better, to get better. Both Martha Washington and Paul demonstrate that happiness is a choice; it is a choice

---

[71] http://izquotes.com/quote/193742

[72] Philippians 4:10-13, The Message Bible

to believe the best is yet to come, even if you don't have tangible proof of it.

You should be ecstatic to know that when you put your heart into your project and win, you can bask in the afterglow of knowing you worked hard; you persevered through the tough parts and came through a winner

Winners are happy people who face their problems with cheerfulness and enthusiasm. They see them less as problems and more as challenges to figure out and overcome. Problems will occur because that's life. Nevertheless, happiness exudes not so much from doing what you like to do, but from liking what you have to do.

When you have a winning attitude, it's easy to find happiness in such things as a baby's smile, a bird's song, or the smells of nature. Well, it's easy for most people to find happiness in those things, but there are a few people who would find something negative even in them. French courier Francois de la Rochefoucauld said, "Few things are needed to make the learned person happy, but nothing satisfies the fool."

Happiness is something most of us strive to find and keep, even when it seems elusive. Of course, nobody is happy all the time; however, some people are happier than others. Happy people choose to find the silver lining in the disappointments life deals them and continue moving forward. These are the people who win in the end.

Be Original

Be honest. Have you ever said to yourself or a confidant, "If I were more like … I know I would succeed"? Or have you ever tried to follow someone else's path toward greatness, although it went against your God-given disposition and was contrary even to what you believed you were supposed to do? It's easy to try to do "it" someone else's way, especially when we cannot see the results from our own way, and that person seems to be winning. One of the most important things you can do for yourself and others is to be yourself. Be original.

No two people are the same. We are all unique in our own way; thus, you should never pretend to be someone you're not or try to be a clone of the person you think has it all. Take pride in being you. When you accept who you are and follow your own dreams, you will be a winner in whatever you do. Take what you have and what you know and always strive to be better. Of course, it's great to have a mentor who can guide you based on his or her own experiences and measures of success, but he or she isn't in your life for you to mimic.

Here's some food for thought on nurturing the unique you God created:

Know your potential. Never second guess yourself or your value. You have more than enough knowledge and talent to achieve your dreams. If you never hear it from another soul, please take it from me: you have what it takes to do whatever you are trying to accomplish. You are well-equipped. Life is too short for you to waste valuable time wrestling with doubt and questioning your identity and worth. You are valuable! You are a winner! "You don't become good by trying to be good. But by finding the goodness that is already within you." ~Eckhart Tolle

Know your spiritual heritage. Faith is confidence or trust in a person or thing or a belief not based on proof. That's a dictionary definition of the word. A biblical definition of "faith" is this: "Faith shows the reality of what we hope for; it is the evidence of things we cannot see." [73]

You must believe in what you're doing, especially if you are a Christian because faith is our heritage. You will not accomplish anything if you don't possess the confidence you'll be victorious. And that confidence comes from being grounded in knowing your spiritual foundation. That's why having a relationship with God sets a firm, immovable foundation for winning in life. Winners are set in what they believe and know their faith is a shield against all distractions that would arise to keep them from excelling. And it doesn't take much to activate. "If you have faith as small as a mustard seed, you can say to this mountain, move from here to there, and it will move. Nothing will be impossible for you." ~Jesus Christ

Know your strengths and weaknesses Self-motivation is probably one of the hardest traits to come by and build on for people who don't read self-help books, particularly if those people are prone to negativity. But knowing what motivates you is something you must unearth before you can maximize your abilities. Your strengths are the keys to your success. Winners know what they can and can't do, and what they need to improve. "When it comes to the best

---

[73] Hebrews 11:1, The Message Bible

way to leverage your ability, it's best to go through your strength." ~ Todd Kashdan

Know your purpose. No matter how badly we want to win, or what we're trying to achieve, we cannot lose sight of our ultimate purpose: to do God's will. We were created by God and for God, and His purpose for us is to impact the lives of other people in such a way that He gets the credit. "I want them back, every last one who bears my name, every man, woman, and child Whom I created for my glory, yes, personally formed and made each one." ~God, via the prophet Isaiah

Be Alert

One of the most pivotal experiences in my life was losing my wife. When she died, she left me alone to raise three young boys as a single parent. It was devastating in the least because I loved my wife, and my children needed their mother. But the situation caused me to develop a deeper level of sensitivity and taught me that we could never take life for granted. Through my pain, I discovered the mystic power of silence and the inner voice of intuition. That's why I can now identify with the hopes, fears, and longings of others. My great loss made me a better person, and as a result, I seek to understand and help others whenever I can.

Successful people maintain a sense of oneness with life by staying mentally alert to everything around them. They are curious, observant, and imaginative. It has been said that "when an opportunity comes your way, you should take advantage of it because you might not get another chance." Nevertheless, if you're not alert, you just might miss a golden opportunity. Alertness will prevent the unpreventable; it will cause the mind to react to its surroundings. In other words, if you are alert, you will take the time to note what's happening around you.

When you take the time to stretch your senses by listening, looking, and comprehending, you will not miss an opportunity when it comes your way. Be alert and stand in awe and wonder of life's unexplained mysteries, and seek to build an ever-increasing bank of knowledge about the world in which you live. "We need to find God, and he cannot be found in noise and restlessness. God is the friend of silence. See how nature—trees, flowers, grass, the moon and the sun, how they move in silence…. We need silence to be able to touch souls." ~Mother Teresa

Be Grateful. Every fourth Thursday in November, families and friends throughout the United States gather around the dinner table to feast on a great spread of turkey, dressing, green beans, cranberry sauce, and pumpkin pie. We also take note of the things we are thankful for. But being grateful and showing appreciation isn't reserved just for Thanksgiving Day.

One of the first things we were taught to say is "Thank you." Can't you hear your mother saying, "Now what to do you say?" after a friendly neighbor hands you a tasty treat. Yes, learning how to say "please" and "thank you" was one of our earliest lessons on gratitude. There's a reason "please" is considered the magic word: it often gets us what we need or want. Thus, having a genuine attitude of gratitude can guide us toward a winning course. And it's not only about what we say, but gratitude is also about what we do.

Gratitude defined is the quality of being thankful, a readiness to show appreciation for and return kindness to.[74] In other words, we are to be grateful for our good fortune and accept our talents and abilities not as entitlements for self-gain but as obligations to be invested for the common good. Gratitude is expressed by our keeping of the golden rule to "do to others as you would have others do unto you."

Show thanks for the beauty of the earth by making it more beautiful. Give thanks for your health and strength by caring for and reverencing your body. Express your gratitude for creative ideas by making contributions to human progress. Demonstrate thanks for each day you're given by living it to the fullest.

We can't take anything for granted. Although we plan for tomorrow, we cannot assume tomorrow is ours. So, we must cherish every moment we've been given, and always show gratitude, toward God and others. Gratitude's cousin is humility, and when we humble ourselves and take note that more than owners, we are stewards of everything God has blessed us with, not just of money but of time, talent, relationships, and even our specific assignments. When we humble ourselves and take on an attitude of gratitude, we'll view our talents and abilities less as resources for self-gain and more as vehicles we use to meet our obligation to invest them for the common good of our communities and beyond. Earlier, I shared with you that I dreamed about writing inspirational books long before I started writing them. My dream was directly tied to my God-given purpose to

---

[74] Looking Back and Looking Forward: Through a Lens Of ..., http://www.breatheministry.com/main/looking-back-and-looking-forward-through-a-l (accessed September 26, 2017).

encourage people to live their best lives. I don't write books to brag about being a published author. No, I want to help people, and that's what you should want to do with your gifts.

Whatever we set out to do in life should be done with the goal of helping others in some way. Even if you want to create or sell a product, that product should be something that helps people and not just put money in the bank. Whatever you do should be done with an appreciation for all you have been afforded by a generous, gracious, and merciful God.

Cultivating Thankfulness. Always express your gratitude, whether it's for something as small as a meal served to you in a fine restaurant, something as big as a large monetary gift, or something as huge as each day you wake up to see a day you've never seen before. Being thankful isn't just about remembering to say "please" and "thank you." It's an attitude, dare I say a lifestyle, which should permeate your very being. Proverbs 3:5-6 is a popular Scripture in the Bible, one many people have memorized. It's often quoted when people need to encourage themselves to keep trusting God despite what they see happening in front of them. It reads: "Trust in the LORD with all your heart; do not depend on your own understanding. Seek his will in all you do, and he will show you which path to take" (NLT).

According to Happify.com, the benefits of expressing gratitude are limitless. "People who regularly practice gratitude by taking time to notice and reflect upon the things they're thankful for experience more positive emotions, feel more alive, sleep better, express more compassion and kindness, and even have stronger immune systems."[75] And conveying your appreciation doesn't have to be reserved only for momentous occasions or holidays. You might express gratitude after receiving a promotion at work or after being served a piece of pie at your favorite restaurant.[76] Another way to nurture an attitude of gratitude in your life is to keep a journal. Making notes of the things you're grateful for can go a long way in improving your sense of self and satisfaction with life in general, according to research conducted by psychologist Robert Emmons.[77] Bottom line: winners are thankful people. "Gratitude unlocks the fullness of life. It turns what we have into enough, and more. It turns denial into acceptance, chaos to order, and confusion to clarity. It can turn a meal into a feast, a house into a home, a stranger into a friend."[78]

Be Friendly

I want to pose a few scenarios, and I want you to honestly answer what your immediate response would be without thinking about it. Here we go:

- A colleague invites you to a networking event he's hosting. You go, but when you walk into the room, you don't recognize anyone and can't find your friend. How do you feel? What do you do?

---

[75] https://my.happify.com/hd/the-science-behind-gratitude/
[76] https://my.happify.com/hd/the-science-behind-gratitude/
[77] https://my.happify.com/hd/the-science-behind-gratitude/
[78] Parrish, Susan. 2016. "The Joy of Gratitude." Columbian, January 3.

- You are part of a tight-knit group of friends that takes an annual trip to a summer home owned by one of the women. This year, one of your friends invites a woman outside of the tight-knit circle to come. How do you feel? How do you respond?
- You've been standing in line for fifteen minutes because the customer in front of you has a cart full of groceries and two of her items require a price check. You're already running late for an appointment. She looks back at you with a nervous smile. How do you respond?

If any of your responses included adjectives like welcoming, approachable, sociable, or gracious, you're a friendly person. But if you were brave enough to admit that you might've been unfriendly to that customer who was holding up the line or less than accepting of the new person who gets invited into your circle of friends, you may need to examine your friendly quotient.

Everyone begins life with a clean slate. Most of us desire to live a life that is worth remembering and something to be proud of. But life's challenges sometimes rob the best of us and cause us to be unfriendly and bitter toward others, especially if we've been hurt. Nevertheless, you must nurture and care for your life with the kind of love and respect it deserves. If someone hurt you, don't allow the pain to define you; don't wallow in it. Seek opportunities to heal in those areas that have been broken in your life, that make it difficult for you to trust others. Ask God to help you with the hard stuff. When you make wise decisions to take care of your well-being, it will lead your life onto a path of happiness and fulfillment.

One of the reasons we shouldn't hold on to the negative emotions like resentment and bitterness is our lives on Earth won't last forever. They aren't meant to. So, we must make the most of our time here. We must take care of ourselves physically, spiritually, and emotionally. Remember, what you put into life is what you're going to get out of it. Recall these few words from the book of Proverbs, "One who has unreliable friends soon comes to ruin, but there is a friend who sticks closer than a brother.[79] Choose your friends wisely, but also be a good friend—the kind that's like family.

The only way to have a friend is to be a friend.

Real friends don't discourage others when they share their dreams; they respond positively, offering insight where they can and encouraging them to never give up on their dreams. Real friends are also honest, even when the feedback they offer may not be something you want to hear. Real friends are sincere. Real friends offer tolerance, embracing differences. Real friends don't hold on to petty grudges; they forgive and move on. If those are the kinds of things you need and look for in your relationship that is what you must extend. Good, healthy friendships enrich your life and can help you realize your dreams. Your friends become your cheerleaders, and you theirs, as you nudge each other toward success.

Always remember that friendship is more than just offering a kind smile or an outstretched hand. It's the spiritual inspiration people receive after discovering someone believes in them and is willing to trust them as a friend. Winners are friendly people. "Friendly people are caring people, eager to

---

[79] Proverbs 18:23, NIV

provide encouragement and support when needed most." ~Rosabeth Moss Kanter

Be Confident

What is self-esteem? "In sociology and psychology, self-esteem reflects a person's overall subjective emotional evaluation of his or her own worth. It is a judgment of oneself as well as an attitude towards the self."[80] Self-esteem is a critical component to one's outcomes. It can determine whether you succeed or fail at something. A low opinion of yourself can leave you feeling defeated or depressed, and the choices you make will reflect just how little you value yourself. That will cause you to fall short in living up to your full potential.

By maintaining a positive and uplifting attitude toward yourself, you will carry a healthy mindset and approach to any given situation. Lilly Singh said, "Love who you are, embrace who you are. Love yourself. When you love yourself, people can kind of pick up on that: they can see confidence, they can see self-esteem, and naturally, people gravitate towards you."[81]

If you struggle with confidence—and most people have some area of insecurity they wrestle with—the first thing you need to do is to choose to love yourself, everything about

---

[80] https://english.my-definitions.com/en/define/self-worth

[81] Lilly Singh Quotes - Brainyquote, http://www.brainyquote.com/quotes/quotes/l/lillysingh743803.html (accessed September 26, 2017).

yourself. Are you perfect? Of course not! But no one is. More than a feeling, love is a choice. So, you have to be deliberate about it. Next, examine your thoughts and change your language. These things really go hand in hand. For example, when you make a mistake, if your first thought is "I'm an idiot," make a conscience effort to think instead, "Oops, I made a mistake. I'll be more careful next time." Or be more specific. If you are given an opportunity to work on a challenging project, but your first thought is, "I don't have what it takes to do that," attack that thought. Turn it around by thinking and saying something like, "That's going to be a challenge, but I'm always up for learning something new." And then you should declare aloud, "I can do all things through Christ, who strengthens me." Taking on a challenge in and of itself is one way to boost your self-esteem. Sometimes you have to act the part until you truly fill it.

Having confidence in yourself is extremely important for success in every aspect of life. If you lack confidence, it will be difficult to make your dreams come true because you'll always be stalled by doubt and fear and will project that in your posture. Most companies are reluctant to invest in an idea that's being pitched by someone who is nervous, fumbling, and overly apologetic. Norman Vincent Peale said, "Believe in yourself. Have faith in your abilities. Without a humble but reasonable confidence in your own powers you cannot be successful or happy." It's much easier to be persuaded by someone who speaks clearly, who holds his or her head high, who answers questions assuredly, and who readily admits when he or she does not know something. By being confident, you can in turn inspire confidence in others. Your friends, your colleagues, your boss, and your customers will be so appreciative when you're confidence shines. And of course, gaining the confidence of others is unlocks the door to success.

Here is the good news: confidence is not an innate trait or something you must be born with. You can learn how to be more confident and continuously build on it until you are 100 percent secure of who you are.

Be Optimistic

Simone Biles is one of the most decorated gymnasts on the world stage. She won five medals at the 2016 summer Olympic Games (four of them gold); she was named Woman of the Year by ESPN; Female Athlete of the Year by the Associated Press; the International Sports Press Association (AIPS) Female Athlete of the Year; the United States Sports Academy Female Athlete of the Year; and the Laureus World Sportswoman of the Year.[82] It goes without saying that she is a winner. But perhaps even more wonderful than her powerhouse tumbling and magnificent uneven bar routines are her bubbly disposition, bright smile, and unassuming personality, which had an infectious impact on her teammates. Here's a lengthy expert from Thecouchgymnast.com about Biles's quick rise in her sport. Pay close attention to the very last line.

> "In the past year, Simones routine had gone from outstanding, to breathtaking. She vaulted her 2 ½

82

https://usagym.org/pages/athletes/athleteListDetail.html?id=164887

> twisting Yurchenko with ease, and a smile was plastered on her face prior to every stuck landing. On beam and bars, her confidence increased with each hit routine, while on floor, she merely skipped into her massive Silivas (double twisting double back) and Biles (double layout half out).
>
> However, what stood out to spectators, judges, and coaches alike was her personality. Simone lit up every arena with her beaming smile. While most competitors remained stoic in concentration, Simone fed off her own positive energy, and her teammates and competitors did as well.
>
> In Nanning, Simone—along with her best friend and teammate Kyla Ross—led an inexperienced US team to the top of the podium on the biggest stage, and most noticeably, the girls seemed like they were having a great time. They were cool and calm while performing, and the team support was infectious: there were high fives and smiles all around. One can't avoid thinking that Simone's optimism was a factor.[83]

Biles embodies all the attitudes a winner should possess: friendliness, confidence, alertness, optimistic, and gratefulness.

Biles humility and graciousness may have a lot to do with her backstory. Her biological mother struggled with drug and alcohol addiction when Biles was much younger, and as a result, Biles and her siblings were in and out of foster care until her maternal grandfather and his wife stepped in and

---

83 http://www.thecouchgymnast.com/2014/10/26/not-just-about-the-medals/

adopted her and her sister when Biles was six years old. Biles could've allowed the darker period in her life to define her, but she didn't. She fulfilled her dreams in spite of it, with a great support system in her parents, whom she often credits for her success.

For Biles, that adoption meant everything because it changed the course of her young life, and she believes it made the difference in her becoming a winner. In a Proctor & Gamble marketing campaign, appropriately named "Thank You, Mom," Biles said about her adoptive mother: "She encourages me and never lets me feel down about something for too long. If I've had a bad day in the gym or needed emotional support, she was always there."[84]

If you don't look on the bright side of things, you won't get far in life. If you tend to see a half empty glass, beginning today start focusing on what's in the glass. Don't focus on what you lack, but work with what you have and keep working until you're exactly where you need to be to reach your goal. Remember this: winners are hopeful even when facing their darkest moments. Winners possess an optimism that compels those around them to get on a winning track. Winners work hard and never give up. Winners have a great attitude.

---

[84] http://www.cnn.com/2016/04/27/health/simone-biles-olympics-mom-100-days-until-rio/

Chapter Eight: Living Your Best Life

"Whatever you want to do, do it now! There are only so many tomorrows."

~Pope Paul VI

One of my favorite parables is a story Jesus tells his disciples about investment. You may know it as the Parable of the Talents. In my paraphrase of the parable, I will call the man a "businessman" and the servants "employees." So here it goes.

> One day, a businessman prepares to take a trip. But before he leaves, he gives three of his employees an assignment (but with different levels of responsibility) to complete while he's away. He gives the first employee $5000 to invest, the second $2,000 to invest, and the third $1,000, according to their abilities. In other words, their assignments were given to them based on their experience and skill set. So, the employee who received the most money to invest was expected to yield the biggest return for his boss—and that's exactly what happened. When the businessman returned home from his long trip (so the employees had plenty of time to complete their assignment), he sent for his employees to report on their progress or outcomes. Just as he expected, the first employee had doubled his investment to $10,000. The second employee also performed well, increasing his amount to $4,000. They each got a promotion. "Good work!

> You did your job well. From now on be my partner," he tells them both.[85] When the third employee gave his report, the outcome was entirely different. He didn't invest the $1,000 he received, and his reason was this: "I know you have high standards and hate careless ways, that you demand the best and make no allowances for error. I was afraid I might disappoint you, so I found a good hiding place and secured your money. Here it is, safe and sound down to the last cent" (24-25). He expected his boss to be pleased with his carefulness, but the businessman's response was the opposite. He exploded. "That's a terrible way to live! It's criminal to live cautiously like that! If you knew I was after the best, why did you do less than the least? The least you could have done would have been to invest the sum with the bankers, where at least I would have gotten a little interest" (26-27). The businessman promptly fired him (in the Bible, the servant is cast into utter darkness) and gave his $1000 to the employee who took the greatest risk and had the highest return on his investment.

The fear of failure can stop you dead in your tracks, especially if you can't see a mistake as an instrument of growth. The employee who did nothing with what he was given was afraid of letting his boss down if his investment choices failed. Some people do nothing with their God-given talents and instead try to be something they're not because it's safer and less risky. However, the only way to be in control of your destiny is to be who you truly are; the only way to live your best life is to pursue the desires of your heart and strive to be the person that

---

[85] Matthew 25:14-30, The Message Bible

you want to be. Invest in what the Creator has given you for a great return. Remember, the talents and dreams you have indeed belong to Him, so you are obligated to invest them.

Living your best life is about facing your fears and taking risks to yield the greatest return on God's investment in you. So how do you live your life to the fullest? You have to manage your fears, create a plan, get organized, develop patience, learn how to smile even when it hurts, love others, and love yourself. When you've given your all, you can be at peace with yourself.

We all want happiness, joy, and peace in our lives. And we don't want just any kind of peace. We want that kind of peace that settles our hearts and minds when we don't have a clue what's happening. One cannot truly live life without that peace that surpasses all our understanding. And to acquire that peace is to be in control. Being control is the key to that peace to living life to the fullest.

Managing Your Fears

I love this quote by Pope John XXIII: "Consult not your fears but your hopes and your dreams. Think not about your frustrations, but about your unfulfilled potential. Concern yourself not with what you tried and failed in, but with what is still possible for you to do."[86]

Challenges and disappointments are a part of life. You get a lukewarm performance review on your job, a promising prospect falls through, you lose all your savings on a business

---

[86] https://www.brainyquote.com/quotes/quotes/p/popejohnxx109443.html

venture with a friend, or your manuscript gets rejected by yet another editor. Perhaps the challenges and disappointments you face are more personal: you're at your wit's end with your rebellious teenager, you're caring for an elderly parent with dementia, your marriage is on the brink of divorce, and you are drowning in debt. The point is no one can avoid the trials of life. While there are some things we can prevent with a lot of hard work, there are other situations that are completely out of our control. But what is in our control is how we respond to those trials. Our fear, that tricky emotion, if not kept in check, can keep us stuck at ground zero or worse, cast into utter darkness!

Let's break down what it means to be afraid.

First, fear is a natural emotion all living beings express when they sense danger around them. That's when fear can be a good thing, as it causes you to get out of harm's way. For example, if you're crossing a busy intersection, you're generally alert. If a car is speeding toward your direction, traveling faster than the speed limit, your natural fear of being hit by it will cause you to quickly get out of the path of danger if you've already started to cross or wait until the car goes by to start walking. However, when we don't take advantage of opportunities that can help us grow and realize goals we have set for ourselves because we don't want to fail or risk rejection, fear becomes a roadblock to fulfilling our dreams.

Now does that mean you will never feel fear in the face of a challenge? Of course not! If you want to be a winner in life, you will face challenges and obstacles, and that doesn't mean you won't ever feel afraid. We all have fears. The point is that you need to confront your fears with a positive, hopeful mindset and armed with God's promise that you can do all things through Jesus Christ, who gives you strength to endure the test because that's all a challenge is—a test.[87]

If you intend to live life to the fullest, you must be willing to accept the challenges that will inevitably come with it. Enthusiastically seek adventures that fearful, more cautious people tend to avoid. Winners confront their fears while losers avoid them. That's the primary difference between the two.

Ultimately, we are responsible for our own lives. And as mature adults, we must take charge of our lives without excuse. Making excuses for mistakes and failure is one of the primary reasons one does not fulfill his or her destiny. When we continually make excuses for not moving forward and complain about what we lack in resources, skill, or time, we waste God's time—yes, that's right, the time you think belongs to you actually belongs to Him. We also make fear an authority in our lives. We end up holding ourselves back when we give in to fear and have only ourselves to blame for not making it happen.

Living life should push you beyond your trepidation. One way to start overcoming your fear of failure (because that's what it's really about) is to accept that disappointment is a part of life. That's right: failure is a part of the growth process. And if we allow ourselves to embrace failure as part of the process, we can become even better because of our mistakes. Realistically, you may not be successful in everything you do. We've already established that Michael Jordan is one of the greatest winners we know, and that's because he never gave up, never ceased to believe in himself—even when he failed. Perhaps what's most important is that he wasn't afraid to fail.

[87] Philippians 4:13

When you set out to accomplish anything, whether it's becoming the best player on your team or earning an advanced college degree, your objective must be to do your best, make the most of what you have, accept what comes, and always give 100 percent effort at everything you do. Make every failure a step toward your success. Take any detection of what is false and allow it to push you toward what is true. When you do those things, fear won't have any chance of getting the upper hand in your life. Instead, success becomes imminent.

Author Shanon Grey says this, "Your life is a book; make it a bestseller."[88] You are the author of your life. You are the one writing every piece of this work, so face every obstacle that intimidates you and don't stop writing until you've made it a bestseller. Or in the words of Nike, "Just do it."

Take Your Time

If you want to win in this fast-paced and challenging world, you have to be patient. We talked about the importance of having a patient "attitude" earlier. Take your time. I'm not talking about the patience that requires you to be still and do nothing but the patience to know success takes time. As you wait, educate yourself. Research blogs dedicated to the topic of your goal. For instance, if you want to write and publish books, search for popular blogs that offer tips on everything involved in writing and publishing your book, from researching ideas to writing inspiration, to marketing. You should also study and incorporate the techniques and methods

---

[88] https://www.goodreads.com/quotes/452084-your-life-is-a-book-make-it-a-bestseller

of highly successful people, particularly those who have succeeded in an area you want to grow in. Note the processes that worked for them, but at the same time learn how to adapt those methods to your unique personality and habits.

Also during this waiting period, set smaller goals you can accomplish in less time. Small victories are great fuel for continuing the journey toward the bigger goals. Waiting will also give you time for self-evaluation. During this period, you can identify things in your life that may be impeding your success, and then learn how to remove them in a calm, cool, and collected manner.

I know waiting is not easy. We live in such an impatient world; people can barely wait thirty seconds for a red light to turn green, so waiting for something that takes a long time to cook is a big challenge. At the same time, you cannot spend all your time in limbo waiting for your breakthrough. So, you must learn the art of working and waiting patiently at once. When you do that, you're not like a kid sitting in the window on Christmas Eve waiting for Santa Claus to show up. You're focused on the task at hand, which you know is leading you to the bigger goal. Before you know it, success will soon be knocking at your door. Joyce Meyer said, "Patience is not simply the ability to wait; it's how we behave while we're waiting."[89]

After my wife died, I was waiting for someone to come to my rescue. I was depressed and ready to give up. But I quickly realized if I didn't accept my situation (after all, there was nothing I could do to change it) condition my mind, build a support team around me, and define my new norm, that I

---

[89] https://www.brainyquote.com/quotes/quotes/j/joycemeyer567645.html

couldn't move forward. I wrote about that experience in my book *Life Is What You Make It: Seven Steps to Moving Forward*. What I'm trying to get you to understand is this: while you're waiting patiently, make it a productive time by doing something that will firmly place you in a winning position.

Smile Even When It Hurts

Smiling comes easy when you're in love, when you get a raise, or when you're sitting around the dinner table enjoying a good meal and great laughs with old friends. But what about when your boss is giving you a hard time on your job day in and day out, when your doctor gives you test results you were not hoping for, or when you're trying to pick up the pieces after a major loss?

Being able to live through difficult moments, no matter how hard, is highly dependent on your outlook on life. As I mentioned just a few sentences ago, I was extremely depressed after my wife passed away. My family and friends did their very best to keep a smile on my face; their love and care saw me through many nights of pain and loneliness. But I had something to live for: my three sons. Knowing that I had to care for them and be at my best emotionally, mentally, and physically gave me a sense of hope and a reason to smile even through my sadness. Because I got through that incredibly dark season, I can say with great confidence today that success in any situation is attainable for you and me.

Living your best life requires infinite smiling! Being able to smile at all times, or better said, being able to laugh through good and bad times, strengthens you. There's even a proverb that backs this up: "A cheerful heart is good medicine, but a crushed spirit dries up the bones."[90] If you don't learn how to smile even through life's darkest moments, trust me—your grief and disappointment will swallow you whole. So, the key is finding that something, searching through the dust of disappointment to find that one shining stone of hope that reminds you there is life beyond the tears and that the tears you shed will only make you better and more prepared to handle what comes with being in the winner's circle of life. My "something" happened to be my sons.

Having something to smile for will give you the relief you need from the stress of life; it is the perfect antidote to anxiety and depression. Having something to smile for allows the sun to shine through the cloudiness of a gloomy day. It will allow you to laugh along with others and not at them. English essayist Charles Lamb wrote, "A laugh is worth a hundred groans in any market."[91] Having a sense of humor helps you to maintain a proper perspective of what's important and what's not.

You shouldn't ponder on a negative situation for long. When you do, the anger you may feel about it can harden into bitterness. Then nothing is humorous to you; nothing brings a smile to your face. The longer you harbor that negativity in your spirit, the harder it will be to smile or find joy in the simple things in life. I believe that's why we are admonished not to hold on to anger. "Do not let your anger cause you shame, nor allow it to last until the sun goes down."[92]

---

[90] Proverbs 17:22, NIV
[91] https://www.primoquotes.com/q/995305
[92] Ephesians 4:26

It has been proven repeatedly that laughter is an excellent way to bring people together. Comedian Victor Borge, who has made a successful living telling jokes, said, "Laughter is the shortest distance between two people." Smiling will add a spring to your step and a glimmer of hope in your eyes. It will tell those around you, "I can overcome this and accomplish the impossible."[93]

Get Organized

Do you have a plan for where you're headed? Do you know what steps you need to take? Have you taken inventory of the resources you have and the resources you need to acquire? Winners have a plan for getting where they want to go, and they know how to achieve the desired result with the minimum use of resources, time, and effort. If you want to win, then you must plan to win—that's what winners do.

Write a personal mission statement. When you set out to accomplish a goal, writing a personal mission statement is a great way to create a physical reminder for yourself of what your purpose is and how you will carry it out to reach your goals. In an article he wrote for Forbes.com, businessman Patrick Hull says that everyone should have a personal mission statement and that it should answer these four questions: what you do, how you do it, who you do it for, and what value you bring to it.[94] A personal mission statement should speak to who you are and how you will approach every

---

[93] https://www.quotev.com/story/7516875/Realistically-speaking/17
[94] https://www.forbes.com/sites/patrickhull/2013/01/10/answer-4-questions-to-get-a-great-mission-statement/#5fa7b46a67f5

area of your life, whether it's your career, your relationships, your spiritual life, and so on.

Set your goals. Over years of observation, I've come to realize that successful people know that creating a formal plan for their goals, what they want to set out to accomplish (establishing objectives) and how they will meet those goals (developing efficient methods) will make any task easier, agreeable, and successful. Such plans include detailed steps to reaching your goal, target dates, and outcomes. The purpose of the plan is to help you stay on track with your specific goals and examine your progress along the way. Winners work hard at finding the most efficient way of getting things done without taking any shortcuts. And if they can't find a way, they will make one.

Practice, Practice, Practice. "Practice makes perfect" is a familiar adage. And it's true! The more you do a thing, the better you get at it. And eventually, you'll become a master of it. If you notice, most successful people practice doing something for a while because they know eventually it will get easy. Once it becomes easy to do, they will enjoy doing it. If they enjoy doing it, they will do it more and more. And if they do it more and more, it will eventually become a habit that helps them reach success.

That pattern of practice is most visible among athletes. They will practice one play until they feel they're ready to run it in real competition. During the game, they know the play backward and forward and know what to do when the play is called. This concept nearly always produces winners. Practice doesn't just make perfect. Practice builds your strength and your confidence. Practice is everything when it comes to winning.

Get Out of Your Comfort Zone

Acting on what you don't yet see can be uncomfortable and downright scary. If you feel that way, guess what—you're normal. I remember when I first started writing inspirational books. Part of my marketing strategy was to give radio interviews, and in the beginning, I was awkward. It was completely out of my comfort zone to sit down with someone and talk about myself and my book in such a public format. However, I had to force myself to do it because it was relevant to what I was trying to accomplish through my work. Today, writing books and giving radio interviews are second nature to me.

Getting out of your comfort zone isn't easy, especially if you are reserved or introverted by nature. But it takes courage and faith to believe that you're walking toward your God-given purpose. If you feel your goal is tied to what God would have you to do, then know that He often sends people into uncomfortable situations. He told Abraham to leave his country and his family and go to a land He was going to show him—later (Genesis 12:1). He sent an insecure Moses to Egypt to rescue the Israelites from slavery—and He told him it wasn't going to be easy because Pharaoh wouldn't let them go without a fight (Exodus 3). When Jesus was approached by a wealthy young man who wanted to know what he had to do to gain eternal life, Jesus told the man to sell his belongings and give to the poor, and that he would have treasure in heaven. But the man didn't want to give up his earthly possessions and chose to walk away (Mark 10:17-22). The man didn't have the faith to let go of temporary riches to inherit eternal riches.

The writer of Hebrews defines faith as “the confidence that what we hope for will actually happen; it gives us assurance about things we cannot see.”[95] Not only could Abraham not see the land God was going to give him, but also, he had no idea where God was leading him. However, he had faith that God would fulfill that promise. So he went. Moses was nervous about what God was sending him to do. He even questioned God’s choice of him when he declared he couldn’t speak that well to face Pharaoh with such demands. But he went, and you know the rest of the story.

I liken getting out of your comfort zone and stepping out on faith to building a business. You must build that business with the mindset of what’s going to happen. When you cannot see the outcome physically, you must see the future result in your mind as you continue building. The process can be uncomfortable, especially when you take a loss or just break even in that first year, but you don’t focus on that. You know that it’s par for the course. In other words, you don’t settle on present occurrences. Whatever happens as you’re building is not a problem because your goal is finishing the project. And if it’s a small business, it can have several “finish” points. The first could be opening the doors for business. The second could be reaching a certain income mark. The third could be introducing a new product. And so on. So, what you must do is take your hope for the future, add a little substance, which is actually called faith, and use it as an assurance that your project is already finished—you’re just going through the process. And in the end, you will have what you’re hoping for, which is to be successful and to become a winner.

---

[95] Hebrews 11

Successful people have a limitless vision; they see infinite possibilities for growth and achievement. They have curiosity and a thirst for adventure, which prompts them to seek and experience new things, things outside of their comfort zone. Truly adventurist people don't have a comfort zone, at least not the way we typically understand it. They think differently from the people who play it safe.

Determine to be a bit more adventurous as you pursue your goals and strive to become the winner God has created you to be. And if you need a physical reminder to step out of your comfort zone when it comes to achieving your goal, write this Brian Tracy quote on an index card, in your journal, or atop your mission statement in bold type as a reminder to never get too comfortable:[96]

> "Move out of your comfort zone. You can only grow if you are willing to feel awkward and uncomfortable when you try something new."

Show Love

You may be wondering what love's got to do with taking risks and living your best life. It has everything to do with it.

No matter what kind of goal you set in life or what resources you use to reach it, if you don't do it from a place of love for others, it won't amount to much in the end. Love is the greatest gift God has invested in us (1 Corinthians 13:2). There is a quote I like. In essence, it says we must love with

---

[96] https://www.brainyquote.com/quotes/quotes/b/briantracy391332.html

great care and courage because loving others requires us to be our most vulnerable selves. And I think that's what pursuing your goals and pressing through uncomfortable situations to reach them is all about—being vulnerable. But know that vulnerability does not equal weakness. Brene Brown even suggested that there is power in vulnerability in a TED Talk.[97] But I want to get back to the notion of love being a part of the equation of success.

To be successful requires being rich in respect and love and being free from envy and hate. Yes, you need to feel good about the success of others and show a great generosity of heart. And you may think this sounds crazy, but it's always better to love than to be loved.

So, what is love?

I like the Bible's for the definition. "Love is patient and kind, love does not envy or boast, it is not arrogant or rude, it does not insist on its own way, it is not irritable or resentful, it does not rejoice at wrongdoing, but rejoices with the truth. Love bears all things, believes all things, hopes all things, and endures all things. Love never ends." [98] All of the characteristics of love are the traits of being a winner. Winners are patient and kind. Winners are humble. Winners don't bulldoze their way toward a goal, knocking down anyone who gets in their way. Winners are not jealous or resentful of those who do just as well or better than them. Winners don't take delight in the shrewd dealings of others. Winners operate in integrity. Winners know how to endure. Winners walk in faith

---

[97] https://www.ted.com/talks/brene_brown_on_vulnerability/up-next
[98] 1 Corinthians 13:4

and hope. Mahatma Gandhi says this about love, "Where there is love, there is life."

Love Yourself

In the previous section, I talked a lot about loving and valuing others as a prerequisite for being a successful person. However, if you don't love yourself, you really won't be able to love others in an authentic, healthy way.

Believe in your heart that you're equipped to live a successful, high quality life. Love who you are and how God uniquely shaped you. When you love yourself and demonstrate that love by taking care of yourself, believing in yourself, and being yourself, you will impact the world around you more than you can imagine. You will grow and enrich your life. When you truly love who you are, you will find that you are no longer a prisoner to meeting the expectations of others. You won't second-guess yourself, and you'll make room for mistakes. When you struggle to embrace yourself, a mistake can send you over the edge emotionally. Have you ever witnessed someone become devastated after making a mistake and then have a difficult time shaking it off? That's likely a person who struggles to love himself. But a person with a healthy respect for himself will see the mistake for what it is and not view it as proof that he is one big failure.

When you love yourself, you will be focused and decisive. You won't hesitate to go for your dreams. You will have something to live for, fight for, and die for. You will feel a sense of purpose and want to make a difference in the lives of others. The person who chooses to love himself will strive to go beyond his own inadequacies including but not limited to the following:

- any failure to meet his own standards,
- self-deception in the face of temptation,
- choosing the worst when he knows better,
- turning a blind eye to the wrongs committed against others when they don't affect him,
- his failure to see the good in others while overlooking the darkness in himself,
- hardness toward his neighbor's faults but readiness to make allowance for his own, and
- a belief he can only do a small work, while others do great works.

Why do I include an exposition on love in a book about changing the way you think to win in life? I include it because your self-perception and your perception of others are critical components of being the kind of person who wins. How you feel about others, and yourself, plays a significant role in perception. In the rough-and-tumble of life, any given day can bring about confusion, disturbing ambiguities, wild fantasies, or strange affiliations that team up to cause you to question your adequacy, challenge your commitment, or negatively impact your effectiveness. Although each new struggle may be slightly different, it is a struggle nonetheless. It is precisely during these questions and change points, whether they are personal, family, or professional, that you should be reminded that you have a reason to finish the task even when it's high noon in your situation. If loving yourself is something you struggle with, the first thing you must do is choose to love yourself—even if you don't feel that way. More than a feeling, love is an action—it's a choice. Here are some more tips for learning to love yourself:

- Act as though you love yourself. Fake it until you'll make it!
- Renew your attitude regularly. Check your negativity at the door.
- Always seek opportunities to grow and improve.
- Nurture your appearance. If you're not pleased with the way you dress or wear your hair, change it up to boost your confidence.
- Be specific about what you need and want, and tell yourself you deserve it.
- Seek greatness.
- Welcome the disciplining and stretching that comes with striving to be great and see it as a validation that you're worthy of greatness.

Understand that success and learning to love yourself authentically and completely, don't come without challenges from oppositional forces. The main opposition you will face is what we know in Christendom as the enemy. He goes by many names, and He will oppose anything good you're trying to do to keep you from living your best life. In the next chapter, I'll explain the primary tactics he uses to keep you down and how you can recognize and overcome them on your way to fulfilling your destiny.

Chapter Nine: Winning the Battle for Your Mind

"A clear mind heals everything that needs to be healed. It can never be fooled into believing that there is one speck out of order."

~Byron Katie

We can be own our worst enemies. However, when it comes to crossing the finish line, there is another force out there that would like to see us become anything but winners.

Some people believe Satan is a myth, nothing more than a caricature of evil adorned in cute red pajamas with a pitchfork in hand, standing on your left shoulder and egging you on to do something you know you shouldn't. Please don't be lulled to sleep by that image. That's how he wants you to see him, as some puny, harmless being encouraging you to take something or do something you're entitled to.

Know this: the enemy of our souls is real, and his intentions are much more diabolical than tempting you to eat a whole pizza when you're trying to shed a few pounds or to keep the extra change the cashier gave you in error. Just as you have a mission to be a better spouse, write your first book, train for that triathlon, start a small business, or volunteer and give more of yourself, the devil has a mission. His mission is to keep you from having a fruitful relationship with God and from realizing your full potential. And gets worse. Satan is a thief whose chief aim is "to steal and kill and destroy."[99]

The devil is no joke, but we have someone much greater than him. We have Someone who is on our side and has equipped us to resist and overcome every tactic the enemy uses against us. The thing is we must use the tools God has given us to outsmart the enemy, tools like confession, faith, prayer, and hope. The primary place the enemy wages war against us is in our minds. If he can get inside our heads, he has access to the greatest weapon he can use against us—and that's us!

In this chapter, I want to break down some of his favorite schemes to keep you stuck in the start position of life and far from realizing your dreams. And I will offer ways you can recognize his tricks and counter them, so you can stay on pace to finish your race victoriously as you win the battle for your mind.

Indecisiveness

Indecisiveness is that going back and forth on what to do, how to do it, or whether or not to do it. The source of indecisiveness can often be pointed to a fear of making a mistake or a lack of faith in one's ability to make the right choice. If we struggle with it, we can drive those around us crazy. Indecisiveness can be self-defeating, and it can make you look weak to others. Ultimately, the constant wavering

---

[99] John 10:10

between going for it and staying in your comfort zone can be a major inhibitor to success.

The mental battle that occurs when we vacillate between pursuing a goal (going for it) and turning back (deciding you're not cut out for it, or it isn't the thing you should be seeking in the first place) is a perpetual struggle for many of us. It's a fight between fulfilling our desires and feeding our fears: *"I want to, yet I don't want to,"* or *"I can do it" and "Who am I to think I can do that."* Being indecisive confounds the minds of many people, and confused is what the enemy wants you to be because if you're confused, constantly going back and forth in your mind, you won't be able to determine how God is specifically leading you. You won't get the insight from Him you need (James 1:5-8). For example, if you believe one moment that you can achieve whatever you set your mind to, but then doubt yourself the next, you are demonstrating a lack of faith in yourself and the One you believed has called you. "God is not honored by the kind of faith that alternates between optimism and pessimism."[100]

Do you struggle with indecisiveness? Has it plagued your pursuit of success in your career, in your business, in your relationships, and so on? Can you win this battle for your mind? Of course, you can!

Here's the thing: while you cannot control what happens to you, you can control your response. Let's say you return to your office after a two-day training, and you're so excited about what you learned that you pitch an idea to your manager

---

[100] MacDonald, Williams. (Art Farstad, Editor). *Believer's Bible Commentary*. Thomas Nelson Publishers: Nashville, 1995, p. 2219 (commentary on James 1:6-8).

for improving internal communication. But the manager doesn't think it's a good idea. Are you disappointed? Sure, especially if it's something you've been working on for a while. But how you respond to that disappointment is within your control. You manage what you think about it and what you'll eventually do. So, you can either think, "I'm a complete failure" or something catastrophic like that, or you can think something more positive like, "Oh well, they'll love the next idea." Either you can vow to quit sharing ideas for fear of rejection, or you can file away their feedback and be sure to consider it the next time you get an opportunity to present an idea. Indecisiveness is just one of the mind games the enemy plays with us, but someone must win and someone must lose. My desire is for you to be a winner and not a loser.

Another way we can be double-minded is to allow our situation to dictate our mood. For example, we're happy when everything is going our way but miserable when nothing seems to go right. We quickly find the words to pray when we're up, but when we find ourselves in a season of struggle, we tend to neglect prayer because we conclude God isn't listening, or worse that God doesn't care about our struggles. When we have money in the bank, we feel blessed, but when we're broke, we succumb to depression and feel like a failure. Should any trial you experience change who you are or where you're headed? Absolutely not! You are still that winning person before any of those trials descended upon your life.

The lesson we must learn and master as we walk toward our destiny is how to be content whether we're up or down, whether we are prospering or struggling to make ends meet, whether we are in a season of peace or we're struggling to keep it together. And here's why: we can do all things through Christ who gives us strength (Philippians 4:13). The word "do" in that Scripture is translated from a Greek word that means "endure." That means you can survive the storms of life, whether it's a season of financial drought or a letdown in your career. Learning to be content helps us to be single-minded and focused, especially when making decisions.

Distractions

A former business owner opened up to a room of her peers about how she had become distracted and what it had cost her. She started dating someone whom she said, "didn't believe in my business or me." She ended up closing her business, only to end up breaking up with the man.

Anything that keeps you from focusing on the goal before you is a distraction, and the enemy loves to use distractions to get us off track. Because some of the things that distract us aren't necessarily bad things, we often don't see them as such, at least not in the beginning. When that woman first started dating her ex, she was probably floating on cloud nine. You know how we are at the start of a relationship when everything is fresh. Without discipline, we find ourselves putting off working on our dream to invest in that relationship. We spend hours talking or texting when we should be researching our book, writing a business plan for our future company, or even getting the rest we need to keep our minds sharp. By the time the woman noticed serious cracks in that relationship, she was too far in it emotionally.

When you're distracted, whether it's a toxic relationship or something else, your thinking gets cloudy, and you're spending too much time thinking about that person and wondering what's going on with him or her instead of being about your business. Distractions are the result of one of the enemy's mind games. Their purpose is to stop you from reaching your destination. Distractions cause you to become pessimistic when difficulties arise. Imagine the problems the woman in the example above experienced when what she was doing and what she considered herself to be was in direct conflict with the relationship she wanted. Because that person was negative about her business, she eventually became negative about it too.

The distractions in your life will come up against anything positive and productive you are trying to do. They often plant seeds of self-doubt in your mind. Those negative thoughts grow into low self-esteem, a root that can be difficult to destroy when it becomes greatly entangled with your soul. The purpose of a distraction is to kill, steal, and destroy whatever dreams you are trying to accomplish. The distraction gets you to respond to your situation as a loser, not as a winner. In other words, whatever occurs in your life, distraction lures you to focus on it and not the big picture, which is to be successful. That is why it's so important that you always think like a winner and act as though you've already won.

Don't let distractions get the best of you. Don't believe you can't be a winner in life. There is a time for everything, and sometimes you must wait a little while for whatever it is you are pursuing to manifest. Even God emphasizes waiting for the right moment. Distraction knows how you will react if you get anxious while you are waiting for that right time. When you don't hold on, however, you set yourself up to become distracted, and then you will act prematurely.

Have you ever noticed how some people try to justify their misfortune? If they have no money, they may say, "Well, it could be worse. Compared to some people, I'm well off." A statement likes that is evidence of a person accepting his position as "broke" or poor—and that's a problem. It says that settling and just playing it safe is okay. It's far from okay. Now, it's fine to be good with just a little if you don't want much. But if you accept little because you think wealth is out of reach for someone like you, that's a problem. It's a mind game the enemy uses to distract you from seeing the bigger picture.

Having faith in God—the One who created you and gave you a purpose unique from anyone else's—is the way to get over the hump on your quest to become a winner. As I mentioned earlier, you are contending with an adversary whose sole purpose is to prevent you from achieving your goals and dreams. He attempts to get you to believe what you're trying to do is impossible, but he's lying to you because nothing is impossible for God. If you're walking with God and trusting Him for everything you need to achieve your goal, a goal He gave you the green light to pursue in the first place, then you have to know it's going to happen. That's why you must stand firm and not waver in your belief, even when you have setbacks.

Listen: there is no such thing as an impossible task. There is hard work, yes. There is endurance, of course. There are also struggles, but we overcome them when we persevere. You have to endure on your way to becoming a successful person. And remember the struggles are part of your success. They make you stronger and wiser. But impossible? HELL NO! "We were created to lead and lead well; we were designed to crush the enemy—and all those distractions he tosses our way—beneath our feet as we run with patience the race before us. Finally, "we are more than conquerors"—this is our assurance.

Strategies for Winning the Battle

I want to share some strategies you can use to stay focused in your pursuit of excellence and success. Remember, the enemy uses tactics such as double-mindedness and distraction to cause you to give up and quit. But you are not going to do that, right?

Never Quit. I don't care how rough the road gets on your journey toward realizing a dream, never give up. One way to achieve your goals is to begin calling yourself what you aim to be. In the same confidence-building workshop I mentioned earlier, the facilitator, Mel Robbins, invited a woman to the stage who had dreams of becoming a filmmaker. When the woman told Robbins she wanted to be a filmmaker, Robbins told her to stop saying what she hoped to be and to begin saying, "I'm a filmmaker."[101] Likewise, declare you are a winner, not just that you want to be one. And remember, winners never quit. If you quit, you are not going to win.

Be Patient. You may be wondering why I keep telling you to be patient or to take your time. It's because it's that important, and patience is one of the hardest things for us to master. Acting prematurely or moving ahead of the appointed time for your dream to occur can cost you. For example, when a baby is born prematurely, he exits his mother's womb before the standard nine-month period of gestation. Depending on how early he is born, that baby will require special attention and critical care because certain organs will not be fully

---

[101] "How to Break the Habit of Self-Doubt and Build Real Confidence" class with Mel Robbins aired on Creativelive.com, August 30, 2017

developed. That baby won't be able to go home with his parents until he is out of the woods. Some premature babies, if born much too early, may even die because of all the complications. If the enemy gets you to act prematurely, you may have to put in some extra time and effort to get back on track toward your destination. Even worse, you even risk wrecking your dream.

Be Content. The bottom line is this: the trick of destruction is to get you to believe you are not controlling your life. However, after God, you control your outcome. Do not let any situation change you and make you act out of a sense of panic and anxiety, which will only make you feel out of control every time.

Now I want you to open up and share in the space below some of the tactics the enemy has used against your mind. Then share how you plan to overcome those tactics

____

____

____

____

____

Let's move on.

Chapter Ten: First Impressions Count (Shine, Baby, Shine)

"Make the most of yourself, for that is all there is of you."

~Ralph Waldo Emerson

Have you ever been caught in a bad moment by someone you were meeting for the first time? You know, when the negative feelings that boiled up from a previous situation just moments before spills into your interaction with a person you know nothing about and who doesn't know nothing about you, except what she's been told by a colleague: *My friend is a marketing guru, and you should connect with her to talk about helping you promote your business*. Still upset about a sour conversation you just had with someone else, your mind was not clear at that moment; it was clouded by anger and frustration. You weren't expecting a potential client to be calling you so soon after talking to that person. So, you ended up returning the cheery greeting on the other line with a stern, "Who is this again?" That was followed by a few seconds of silence and stammering on the other end before she confirmed she was referred to you, but that time her voice was less cheery and a lot more hesitant. Yikes!

You only have one chance to make a first impression, and a few seconds to make it a good one. Imagine if that exchange had taken place in person. Do you realize that you could've still sent a poor first impression without uttering one word? That's right, because we speak through our body language, our facial expressions, and our appearance, and not just with our words. Often if you don't mean what you say, those are the very things—your body language and your facial expressions—that will betray you. So, as you set out to become a winner, ask yourself this question, "What kind of impression am I making?" Then determine whether it is helping or hindering you.

You can't control how people act or what they do; however, did you realize that you can control what they think and say about you just by the way you conduct yourself? Yes, that's true, and I want to spend a little time talking about how you can shine in your first impressions, particularly in a job interview. I am dedicating this chapter specifically to people who are seeking to move up in their careers, whether it's where you work now or with a new company altogether. But if you're self-employed and looking to increase your pool of prospects and get more clients, this chapter is for you too. If you want to learn how to project an image of confidence and walk away from any situation a winner, I want to share with you how you can make a great first impression.

Even if you don't land the position you're interviewing for, making a good impression will leave a lasting effect on that person you've met with. For example, years ago a high school graduate interviewed for a job with the federal government; however, because she was going away to college that fall, the interviewer could not offer her the position, a permanent, grade-level job. But she left such a good impression with the interviewer that they found an opening for a temporary position with the same title and called her back to offer her that position. She accepted it, and every summer for the next four years, she worked for that agency. When she graduated from college, they wanted her to consider working there permanently, but she chose to find a different job that would align with her dreams and goals. Making a good impression not only opened a door for her, but it also gave her options.

If you want people—in this case, a hiring manager, your boss, or a future client—to think well of you and look at you with admiration and respect, show them that you deserve that level of appreciation and are worth the investment. And it starts with the value you place on yourself. Whatever we deem has value is what we tend to spend more time on. If winning is important to you, then principles, standards, and behavior should be at the top of your priority list.

Believe You Deserve it

How valuable are you to yourself? How valuable do you want to be to others? How valuable are you to the company you currently work for? Winners know the value they bring to the table and that they deserve the position they are trying to land or the promotion they are hoping to get. Take this bit of advice from the late political theorist Hannah Arendt, "Dedicate yourself to the good you deserve and desire for yourself. Give yourself peace of mind. You deserve to be happy. You deserve delight."[102]

You have to prove you deserve to be that person who gets the call to represent the company. Let's say you desire to be hired by a distinguished, purpose-driven corporation—a company that isn't just about the bottom line. First, you need

[102] http://izquotes.com/quote/6554

to know that most purpose-driven organizations endeavor to make a difference in the world, and they want to be distinct from other companies like theirs. They believe giving back is the best thing to do, and they treat their employees well, ensuring they have opportunities to develop their abilities and talents and contribute to the growth of the company. So they are careful about whom they select to interview and particular about whom they chose to hire. You need to make an excellent impression to show that you deserve to work for such a company.

Seeking a purpose-driven occupation implies you also want to give back. It indicates that you like contributing your time, energy, and talents to a noble profession, and you're pleased to tell your family and companions what you do. What's more, to sweeten the deal, these sorts of organizations normally have the best working environments and incentives, emphasizing both fun in the workplace and professional development.

Do you deserve such a job? Well, I believe you do. However, you not only must know that you deserve it, but you must also go out and get it; and it starts with being prepared to make a good impression. Here are a couple of practical tips for landing a purpose-driven job:

1. Know Where to Look

The Internet is taking over everything, including how one conducts a job search. There are job boards like Monster.com and Indeed.com and social media platforms like LinkedIn that have transformed the way people look for work and even how employers and recruiters vet potential hires. Having a good

LinkedIn profile has become just as important, if not more, than having a well-written resume. If you're seeking to work for a company that wants to make a difference in the world, please check out the website Gamechangers500.com. This site features a rundown of the world's top purpose-driven organizations.[103]

Once you decide to apply to a purpose-driven organization, you must ditch the traditional route of sending your resume. That kind of approach won't work with those types of companies. Purpose-driven organizations are the wave of the future, and they require another method, but you will need to keep in mind your end goal, which is to stand out enough to be noticed or make a good impression.

2. Choose a company with a mission that matches yours

Purpose-driven companies look for certain qualifications and attributes in their candidates and hire individuals who are in alignment with their vision and mission. Earlier, I mentioned that you should develop a personal mission statement. When you do your research on the companies you're interested in working for, research their mission and vision statements. Compare them to yours. If you don't have a personal mission or vision statement before you apply, make a list of the things that make a difference to you and what sort of commitment you need to make. Then search for an organization with a similar vision and ensure that you have clarity about what your ideal purpose-driven job position looks like. Knowing that will help you discover an organization that truly fits. Then

[103] https://www.workitdaily.com/finding-purpose-driven-job/

you can utilize your creativity to emerge and land that perfect job.

3. Emerge

Once you determine the organizations that will be the best fit for you, use a unique approach to stand out from your competition. It's clear that purpose-driven organizations need individuals who aren't reluctant to express their qualification, qualities, interests, and values. And with so much information available on the Internet nowadays, it is simpler than any other time in history to do your homework and make a good lasting impression with prospective employers.

Value Yourself

Be proud of yourself, of who you are and what you do. And never apologize for being you or for your station in life. Always handle yourself with pride and respect. People who are insecure may mistake your confidence for arrogance. Now, here is an instance where you do the right thing to make a good impression but because of the brokenness or insecurity in the person you are interacting with, you cannot control what that person thinks. But don't second-guess yourself when that happens. There's a big difference between being sure of yourself and proud of who you are and being conceited and big headed. People who are confident are also humble and have no need or desire to compare themselves to others or make themselves better than others. They want to help others. People who are conceited tend to compare themselves to others to prove why they are bigger, smarter, or stronger—and when they do that, they are just revealing their insecurities.

The answers you give people will say a lot about how you think. For example, let's say you are not working or looking for a better job. When people ask you what you do for a living, how you answer is important. Most people would say something like, "I'm just another unemployed person searching for a job," or they might say "I'm just trying to get a better job, and I'm not having any luck." They focus on the negative aspects of their situation, or they downplay their worth.

Those kinds of answers can leave a negative impression with the interviewer. By describing yourself by your current employment status, you have told the interviewer that you aren't worth their time or consideration. Also, with an answer like that, you demonstrate that you are not giving your all to get what you want. In any search for a new job, new position, or new client, you have to think like a winner and act like you won to get to where you want to be in your career or your business. So instead of those negative answers, you might consider saying something like this, "Mr. Jones, I've been working in this field ten years, and the best thing about being able to do what we do is to make a difference. I am excited to be meeting with you today about how we can work together to further your mission and my growth. I am looking forward to being employed by one of the most distinguished companies in the country, and I know I'm going add value to the business."

You can well imagine the difference in the impression you would make with an answer like that, not to mention the value you create in your mind which says, I'm thinking like a winner, and I'm acting like I already won.

The way you think is the foundation of winning or losing. If you have negative thoughts, you will get negative results.

So, you have to think with optimism so that you can get positive results. According to Denis Watley, the best-selling author of the audio series *The Psychology of Winning*, "The reason most people never reach their goals is that they don't define them, or ever seriously consider them as believable or achievable. Winners can tell you where they are going, what they plan to do along the way, and who will be sharing the adventure with them."[104]

Having the Right Response

It's human nature to show appreciation when someone shows us kindness. However, it is not enough just to be kind to that person who was nice to you. You should show gratitude to everyone who deserves it. And it shouldn't be based on what someone did for you.

When you show someone how much you appreciate him or her, it's almost guaranteed that you will get more out of that person. But if you don't show that kindness, for sure you're probably not going to see a next time with that person, or you will get less out of him or her. Be gracious to everyone. Sincere and genuine kindness will take you far toward being successful in life. No one likes to be taken for a ride. In most cases, people will know when you are real and when you are not, so mean what you say and say what you mean.

Your response is like your access code. If you enter the wrong code, you will never see further than where you are. And if you attempt to enter the code multiple times, you will

[104] http://www.quotationspage.com/quote/3127.html

automatically get locked out of the system. Have you ever forgotten your pin number for your ATM card, and while trying to use your card you accidentally punch in the wrong number multiple times? If this has never happened to you, I can tell you from personal experience what's going happen if it ever does: the machine will automatically suck your card in and sometimes shred it.

How you communicate when you're meeting with decision makers is important. I'm sure you've already heard some of the things I'm about to share with you, but I want to share them again because I want you to land that opportunity; I want you to succeed!

Tips for Responding Well in an Interview or Meeting:

Job interviews or meetings with potential clients can be nerve wrecking. Here are a few pointers for putting your best foot forward:

- **Pay attention to your body language.** Posture is important: make sure you're sitting straight with shoulders squared. Make direct eye contact and relax.
- **Speak clearly**. Don't mumble, whisper, or slur your words.
- **Have confidence in what you know; talk about it with authority.** At the same time, don't pretend to know something you don't—and don't be afraid to admit when you don't fully understand a topic that may come up. Simply say, "I've heard of that; I'll have to look into it more."

- **Mention the person you're meeting with by name.** For example, when you're ending the conversation and thanking the person for his or her time, be sure to say, "Thank you, Ms. Jones." If it's the kind of meeting where first names are allowed (and that is becoming increasingly so), "Thank you, Tammy, for the opportunity to explain how we can work together to make XYZ Company fulfill our mutual missions and grow."

Hopefully, you get what I'm saying. Learning how to respond appropriately in those types of situations may take some time to master. The average person may overlook it. I'll be honest with you: it took me awhile before I realized that how I communicated and answered certain questions in all kinds of situations was an asset to have in my arsenal for acquiring success. Trust me, it's a skill that will benefit you for the rest of your life.

Chapter Eleven: You Are What You Think

"It's not what you are that holds you back; it's what you think you are not."

~Denis Waitley

Have you ever met a fearless person who would probably try anything at least once? That's the kind of person W. Mitchell is. An energetic and adventurous person, when Mitchell wasn't amusing his passengers as he carried them up and down the hills of San Francisco as a cable-car grip operator, he could be found riding his motorcycle or flying his airplane.[105] But his life took a spill—a big one—one night while he out riding his motorcycle. It was cold and wet, the perfect condition for an accident. And that's what happened, but the accident was catastrophic.

When his motorcycle slipped and fell onto the wet ground, his gas tank was damaged. As gas began to leak out, the tank exploded with Mitchell still on the bike. He sustained third-degree burns over sixty percent of his body. It goes without saying that his recovery was long and arduous: he needed help doing everything for a while, and he had to have sixteen surgeries. But the accident didn't keep him down. Not only was he able to return to work, but he also started flying his

[105] www.wmitchell.com

airplane again—just four months after his horrible accident. Can you imagine that? Some people would have been so shell-shocked that they would've been too afraid to get back on a motorcycle, let alone get on an airplane.

Mitchell continued to live his life to the fullest. He had a scarred face and limited use of his hands, but that didn't stop him from going for his dreams or fulfilling his goals. He partnered with a couple of friends to start a wood-burning business that became one of the largest employers in Vermont, creating opportunities for others.

How would you describe this man? Courageous? Umm, yes. A risk-taker? For sure. Determined? Absolutely! Now if you're still wondering if you can overcome your situation or the obstacles in your way to become a winner, please hold on. There's more to his story.

Four years after surviving that harrowing motorcycle accident, Mitchell was flying his airplane, and it crashed, crushing his backbone. Today, he is paralyzed from his waist down. Did Mitchell have incredibly bad luck or was life unfair to him? You would think after that, and after everything he had been through following the motorcycle accident, that he would say, "I've had enough. Life has had it in for me. I'm going to call it a day. I quit."

Not W. Mitchell.

He went on to run for the office of mayor—and he won. He ran for Congress with the slogan "Not just another pretty face." He took up white water rafting, fell in love, got married, and went back to school to earn his master's degree. He didn't stop living his life to the fullest. Today, he is a highly acclaimed motivational speaker who reminds his audiences of this: "It's not what happens to you. It's what you do about it."

The next time you think you can't, think about W. Mitchell. He never thought he couldn't, even after the handicaps. "Before I was paralyzed, there were 10,000 things I could do. Now there are 9,000. I can either dwell on the 1,000 I've lost or focus on the 9,000 I have left."[106]

Nothing stopped Mitchell from being the energetic, quick-witted person he was born to be. Nothing stopped him from being himself. And as a result, he lives a fuller life than many people who haven't lost as much as he has.

Unfortunately, there are many people who think life isn't fair. If a relationship fails or they can't seem to catch a break financially, or they had a difficult upbringing that has colored their outlook even as adults, they tend to go around feeling sorry for themselves. They throw the best pity parties, saying things like, "You've never walked in my shoes, so you wouldn't know what I'm feeling," "My parents weren't there for me" or "Nothing good ever happens for me."

When my wife was sick and incapacitated, I worked two jobs while taking care of her and our children. I did everything I could to keep it all together, but my situation grew worse when she died. I then had to fill the emptiness her departure left for my boys, being both father and mother to them. It wasn't easy. It hurt. I was devastated. But I didn't let it keep me down for long. I couldn't because those three young lives were depending on me. And, as a minister, I had things to do for God and people to serve. I had dreams yet to fulfill. I had

---

[106] ibid

to keep living my life to the fullest—even without my beloved by my side.

Life isn't fair. And don't believe anyone who tries to tell you otherwise. Neither the Bible nor the Constitution of the United States declares it to be fair. So, if you have been going around throwing pity parties, stop right now and begin taking responsibility for whatever life tosses your way. Remember, we cannot control what happens to us, but we can control what we think about it and what we do after it. Think of life as a game of spades. Some people get a great hand, filled with aces and a joker or two. While others are dealt a bad hand, sometimes one that looks like it can't even make board. But if that bad hand is played strategically, it can do a lot more than what appears at first glance. No matter what kind of hand you've been dealt, nothing can prevent you from overcoming adversity and becoming a winner in life—that is, nothing or nobody but you.

So, whenever you're tempted to feel sorry for yourself when, yet another company doesn't hire you after your umpteenth interview, or your doctor gives you some bad news, or you experience another financial setback, or you lose someone you love, or you lose a client, remember Mitchell's story. It's okay to cry at the moment, but you must keep moving. You cannot allow your situation to shape your outlook on the rest of your life or guide your course. Because if you think you're a loser just because something didn't go your way, guess what— you become a loser. It sounds harsh, I know, but it's true.

Taking Risks

Author James Allen wrote, "Man's mind may be likened to a garden, which may be intelligently cultivated or allowed to run wild."[107]

We live in uncertainty, no question about it. As the adage goes, "Nothing in life is guaranteed." Everything you do is a risk. However, we are living in a real world, so we have no choice but to take risks. Whatever you think will override the risk. If you believe you're a winner, the risk will be worth taking.

Many people would say I'm a risk taker because of the time, money, and effort I put into my passion. Compared to the average Joe or Jill, I can see why someone might say that. But one thing you must understand is whatever you think and believe to be your God-given ability is what will make you successful if you use it. So, your only real option is to go for broke.

I get a rush when people tell me things like, "You're a risk taker" or "You're wasting your time; you're not going to be successful." I say to them, "I'm already successful." Having the attitude, or mindset that you're already what you're aspiring to be is what makes you a winner. If you believe it and speak it, you'll be it.

Let's talk about speaking "it" for a minute, because most people don't understand the power of words and how they can impact your dreams. "Life and death are in the power of the

---

[107] www.goodreads.com

tongue."[108] Whatever you think in your heart is what you will eventually become. For example, a middle-aged woman lost her mother to illness when she was just three years old. Her father wasn't in her everyday life because he had challenges of his own. So her grandparents raised her. She grew up comparing her life to her friends who had both parents and yearning for what they had, despite having grandparents who loved her and tried to protect her and give her the things she needed. She ended up getting into all kinds of trouble, but an early pregnancy got her back on track with school. Still, deep down she struggled to see herself as someone who was wanted, and as a result, all her decisions in life were driven by her sense of worthlessness and rejection. Some people began to treat her the way she saw herself, and she would often say, "It's not fair. Why can't I ever have what I want?"

Your words have the power to change your life dramatically. Meditate on that for a moment. Once you begin speaking and those words get into your mind, it becomes difficult to change directions. Our brains are like computers and our words programs. When a negative situation occurs, our brain tells our mouths or minds to play a particular program, and out comes the words that align with the program, which is either a "life sucks" program or "I can and will overcome this" program. But the good news is that you can reprogram your mind if a pessimistic outlook drives your thinking and shapes your thoughts.

Your mind must first be convinced about who you are and what you're capable of doing and achieving before you act because action follows the direction of your thinking. If you

---

[108] Proverbs 18:21

believe you don't have what it takes to grow your small business and earn six figures annually, you won't prospect for new clients or implement a marketing plan to get out the word about what you do. If you don't think you're smart enough to pass your nursing boards after failing it the first couple of times, you won't study harder—or at all—to take it a third time. But if you believe you're the best at what you do, you will act on your belief with your best effort. You'll look forward to doing whatever you do with an eagerness to learn and grow. Whatever you think of yourself will impact the finished product. Action is the process that gets you there.

I know many people are hesitant to take action because of fear of what they think could be wrong. In other words, they are afraid of failure. Afraid of what people may say. Afraid of losing money. Afraid they're already past their prime of attempting anything too risky. But as Albert Einstein would say, "A person who never makes a mistake never tried anything new."[109]

Successful people have the same fears as everyone else. However, after they consider what they could accomplish, they override their fear by taking action. They "think in the morning. Act in the noon. Eat in the evening. Sleep in the night."[110]

Everything we are or will ever become will come because of what's going on in our mind. We cannot achieve our purpose through physical effort alone. The power comes from our thoughts and everything we do to improve the quality of our thinking. As you think, that's what you'll become. The

---

[109] https://www.brainyquote.com/quotes/quotes/a/alberteins148788.html
[110] William Blake

Bible talks about "renewing your mind." That sentiment is counter to what we've been taught, and that hard physical work is the foundation of success. Although we do need to exert ourselves physically, it's important we understand that our thoughts drive our actions. If we have an optimistic outlook, we'll put in the work. If we have a pessimistic outlook, we may procrastinate or make excuses for not doing what we need to do to get to where we want to go.

Once you mentally commit to confidence—choosing to think well of yourself and your ability to succeed at whatever you set your mind to—it will grow and evolve, and your dreams will become a reality. Have you ever noticed how success-minded people always expect the best in all that they do? They create their own expectations to keep themselves consistent with what they want.

Everything in life is a result of sowing and reaping. Everything grows in some aspect. A seed from a plant grows from the nutrition of water and fertilizer. A thought grows as we keep thinking about a situation, and it eventually becomes reality, so if we want to change our reality, we must change our thoughts. How do we change our thoughts? We stop feeding them negative food. We stop feeding them by not continually thinking about the negative things. If we stop continually thinking on it, it will eventually die.

Don't Overthink It

Most of us do our best to stay upbeat, but sometimes we can slip into old habits of thinking negatively about a situation that can cause chaos if we don't cut off those thoughts at the pass. It's what I call overthinking a thing.

We may ruminate on past mistakes and have regrets about things we cannot change. Instead of leaving the past in the past and taking advantage of the opportunity to do things differently and better, we worry about how our past mistakes may negatively affect current situations or lead to negative consequences in the future. We might over-analyze everyday experiences, reading into them things that aren't real. We assume a friend's quiet demeanor means the person is upset with us. As soon as one bad thing happens, we associate it with all the other bad things that have happened in our lives and begin to feel depressed. We struggle to enjoy the present day, as we worry and obsess about everything that could go wrong. When we overthink a thing, we have a hard time getting out of our heads.

If you find yourself in that state of mind often, you are what psychologists call an over-thinker, and this way of thinking can be detrimental to your mental and emotional. [111] Psychologists have found that over-thinking can lead to depression, misery, and fatigue, especially in women, who are much more likely than men to dwell on the experiences that stress and dissatisfy them. Scientific research has shown that women more than men strive for perfection in things they set

---

[111] Psychologytoday.com, "Six Tips to Stop Overthinking," Amy Morin, Feb. 12, 2016

out to do, and thus, beat themselves up a bit more when something doesn't go the way they'd hoped.[112] "When a professional endeavor goes wrong, women are more likely to blame themselves," according to the *Time* article.[113] We can look to the most recent presidential election in which Clinton, the first woman nominated by a major political party, lost the race after she was expected to win. She says of the days immediately following her defeat. "There have been a few times this past week when all I wanted to do was to just curl up with a good book or our dogs and never leave the house again," Clinton shared at a charity event not long after the election.[114] Clinton even wrote a book about her experience, in which she puts much of the blame on herself for her loss. But our tendency to overthink something isn't fueled by negative personal experiences alone.

With so much negative news coverage these days that evoke fear and the growing unrest in society, it's easy for negative thought patterns to take root in our minds. Many people who think negatively are healthy individuals who value relationships and care deeply for the people in their lives. However, without realizing it, they often push away the very people they are concerned about or seek support and encouragement from because they can become preoccupied, fearful, miserable, and hard to be around. There is no switch in the brain that can be quickly turn off over-thinking; it's a habit that requires dedication and hard work to recover from. Here are a couple of ways to stop over-thinking and find peace.

---

[112] Time.com, "It's Not You, It's Science: How Perfectionism Holds Women Back," Jessica Bennett, April 22, 2014

[113] ibid

[114] News.sky.com, "Hillary Clinton admits she wanted to 'curl up' after election loss, Thursday, 17 November 2016, UK

Relax, Relate Release—Breathe. There's a hilarious scene in the old sitcom *A Different World.* In it, Jasmine Guy's character (Whitley Gilbert) goes to see a therapist because she's torn between wanting to be with her current boyfriend, who's super smart but poor, and the jet-setting life her ex-boyfriend has with his soon-to-be wife.[115] True to her high sprung and demanding nature, Whitley agonizes over her situation—having to watch another woman have all the things she wants and wishes she could have with the man she's with. Realizing how wound up (and perhaps a little shallow) Whitley is, the therapist tells her that she has to "relax, relate, release." In other words, she needed to calm down, realize the good thing she already had—even without the riches—and release the past and live in the present. I liken that release to learning how to breathe metaphorically and physically when we find ourselves face-to-face with those things that both stress and stretch us.

Breathing will relax you, calm you, connect you to your task, and help you feel grounded. It sounds simple, but often when our minds start to race toward dangerous places, our first response is hysteria and anxiety. However, that's when we need to relax the body and mind. One way to improve your breathing is to use meditation apps. They are readily available to download on your smartphones or tablet. Daily listening can help ease any anxiety, fear, worry, or doubt that may be plaguing you.

Surrender to God and your purpose. Surrendering does not mean giving up; it just means you are willing to go with the

---

[115] *A Different World*, Season 4, episode 13, "Ex-Communication," directed by Debbie Allen, written by Jeannette Collins and Mimi Friedman, originally aired January 31, 1991

flow—or more accurately, God's flow—which isn't always easy. But it is the only way to go if you want to be successful. Surrendering is a form of release that brings peace to your life because it means you are willing to trust that everything will work out just as it is supposed to.

Psychotherapist Amy Morin offers these six tips for tackling overthinking:

1. **Notice When You're Thinking Too Much.** This will require that you be conscious of your thoughts. Sometimes we don't realize when we're overthinking because we're not aware of ourselves. So how can you do this? Pay attention to when you find yourself replaying a scene in your head, incessantly going over what someone said to you or how you responded to something. If it's a situation you cannot change, decide to stop thinking about it at that moment.

2. **Challenge your thoughts.** Have you ever worked yourself into a frenzy with a "what if that happens" as you contemplate whether or not to do something, and that "what if" is the worst possible outcome? For example, if you have a thought like this: "If I leave my job to freelance full-time, I will end up losing everything because I won't earn enough," what do you think will happen? You'll probably never step out on faith and try to make your dream a reality because not only are you too afraid of failing, but you're also pretty much expecting to fail. Even if failure is a possibility, how can you challenge a thought like, get out of your head, and move forward with a plan in place?

3. **Keep the focus on active problem-solving.** Revisiting the example above, instead of focusing on everything that could go wrong if you quit your day job to work your small business full-time, create a plan for success. A good plan will

make room for setbacks. If your overthinking is the result of a mistake that you made in the past, instead of beating yourself up repeatedly, forgive yourself and figure out what you need to do to keep from making the same mistake again. Remember, forgiving yourself is key—because if you don't, you won't be able to move on in a healthy and real way.

4. **Schedule time for reflection.** We've established that turning a thing over and over in our heads is not good for our psyche or our growth. But a little reflection won't hurt. Morin suggests giving yourself twenty minutes a day to "let yourself worry, ruminate, or mull over whatever you want."[116] But once the twenty minutes are up, be done with that and move on. You can even use the time to determine what you'll do differently the next time to have a better outcome. Above all, you'll move on and try not to revisit it.

5. **Practice mindfulness.** Live in the here-and-now. Leave yesterday in the past. Unless you're God, you cannot turn back the hands of time. And the best thing you can do for yourself is live in the present and think positively about the future.

6. **Change the channel.** Or more simply, do something different. If you're struggling to stop thinking about something that's just making you feel bad, busy yourself with some other activity. Work on a project, call to check on a friend, get up, and exercise.

To combat overthinking, we must be aware of our thoughts because they have power, more than we realize; they can create outcomes we may not want.

---

[116] Psychologytoday.com, "Six Tips to Stop Overthinking," Amy Morin, Feb. 12, 2016

Seize Life

Life doesn't stop for anyone; you have to keep on striving and seeking for what you want. "Ask and it will be given to you; seek and you will find; knock and the door will be opened to you."[117] Those are the words of Jesus Christ. So how do you begin seeking and seizing life?

First, you must know what you want out of your life. What is your purpose? What is your intention? Do you want to be rich or happy? Do you want to be wealthy? Do you want to be successful and not necessarily wealthy? Do you want to have a career or a job? How about money—do you want it or need it? Do you want a house or a home? Do you care about your outcomes or are you like a tree tossed back and forth in the wind and ready to settle wherever life leads you? These are just a few things you need to consider as you set out to adjust your thinking to enrich and grow your life. Bottom line: know what you want, and then get about the business of getting it.

The quality of your life depends on what is inside you. Beauty is more than skin deep, but if you think you're ugly and going to be poor all your life, maybe you are correct. No one can make you do something that you don't want to do. Once again, life is what you make it. So, get something good inside you, and something good will come out.

---

[117] Matthew 7:7, NIV

Believe in What You're Selling

There's a saying, "If you don't stand for something you will fall for anything." In other words, every new thing that comes along you will want to be a part of it; you will believe everything that is being said to you—true or false.

We all are a representation of somebody or something. When you look at yourself in the mirror, who or what would you say you represent? Is it something or someone you would be proud to talk about? When you open your mouth and speak, do people listen with interest? Are you confident about what you're saying?

If a company needs to sell a product, it needs to let consumers know about that product to sell it. One of the ways it does that is through marketing or advertising. An advertisement comes in various forms—billboards, newspaper and magazine ads, and television commercials. Some products have a spokesperson, someone who speaks on behalf of the company about that product or a celebrity who becomes the face of their product. That voice or face you see embodies the company's brand and represents everything that's good about the product, and why it believes its targeted audience should invest in it.

Now think of yourself as a spokesperson that represents a product or a brand. What are you selling or marketing? Yourself. When you open your mouth and speak, would anyone buy what you're saying? From the time you open your mouth or act, others will be able to tell what you're all about and what your intentions are. Are you believable? Are you reputable? Will people support you?

The power of a spokesperson for a product, company, or brand is beyond our imagination. Many of us are spokespeople without even realizing it. For example, if you use a lawn service to treat your grass monthly, that little sign they stick in your yard tells your neighbors or people walking or driving by that you approve of the product and service. If you serve a brand of soda to guests in your home, you're endorsing that brand. If you eat at a certain restaurant, wear a specific brand of shoes, and the list goes on, you are an unofficial spokesperson for that product and the company that creates it. If your name or reputation is associated with something, you want to make sure it's a good product. When a corporation purchases ad space on a television program, it isn't just trying to sell something. It's also indicating their support of the program and its belief in the program's goals and messaging. If something goes awry that brings bad publicity to the program, guess what'll happen? Yes, the company typically pulls its ad because it doesn't want its product associated with the negativity surrounding that program. Or if a celebrity gets bad press coverage after a questionable decision, some of the companies and products associated with that celebrity sever their business relationship because they don't want their brand to be connected to that person.

Know Who You Represent

You may unofficially represent many products, companies, leaders, or organizations you choose to invest or engage in your day-to-day life, but the most important brand or person you represent is you. So, wouldn't you want to be a good representative for yourself? Of course, you would! Who are you representing? A winner? However, you see yourself, and I hope your vision is something life-affirming and aligned with your hopes and dreams for your life, don't let anyone peg you as something you're not. One of the worst things we can do is try to be something others believe we are or think we should be. Don't let people call you a bus driver, but you don't have a license. How could you say you are a pilot if you're afraid of heights, or a lifeguard but you cannot swim? I know some of these examples may sound far-fetched, but my point is this: don't be an inadequate or misleading representation of who you are for any reason. At the same time, don't allow others to define for you what you should look like as a _______________ (you fill in the blank) if that's what you desire to be. Here's a perfect illustration.

For over forty-five years, Jack Peter Mark lived alone in an apartment on the upper side of Brooklyn, New York. Every day, Mr. Mark would make a trip to his neighborhood newsstand to purchase a newspaper. Rain or shine, Mr. Mark was always on time to buy his newspaper each morning. But the interesting thing about him is that he could not read because Mr. Mark is blind, with a seeing-eye dog who guides him wherever he wants to go. One day, someone observing him heading home with newspaper in tow stopped him and asked why he bought a paper every day when he can't see to read it. He replied by saying, "I am the owner of the paper company and the newsstand. I purchase a paper every day, rain or shine, just to show that this paper is so good that a blind person could read it."

Do you get the picture? Who are you? Or better yet, who are you representing, or who do you want to represent? Please share your answer in your journal or the space below.

Do What You Do Best

The great thing about life is that we all have the ability to win. We only need to discover what our talents are and use them to the best of our ability. When you give time and energy to your natural talents, you will reap extraordinary rewards.

Rejoicing in our natural abilities should be an easy thing to do, but for countless people, it's emotionally draining because they fight their giftedness for one reason or another. Perhaps their parents would disapprove of their desire and talent to write or paint because their parents want them to prosper as a doctor or lawyer. Or it could be that a person wants to work for a social service agency because he wants to help people who are disenfranchised, but at the same time, he wants to prosper financially and realizes that a career in social work may not yield him the kind of prosperity he aspires to have.

And then there are those who are too scared to pursue their dreams because no matter how good they are at something, they don't think they're good enough to succeed; too often they are comparing themselves to others or can't accept anything less than perfection. Those are all justifications, but all the justifications in the world won't make natural talent go away. It will be there; a burning desire waiting for us to have faith and move through fear and doubts until we recognize what we should have been doing our whole lives. We have been given a purpose, through our natural talents and gifts, for a reason—to use them for the advancement of the world and those who live in it.

Have you ever observed that when you participate in an activity in which you are naturally gifted, you feel invigorated, enthusiastic, and positive? That's an indication that those are the things you should be concentrating on—when you're nearly buzzing all over, so happy you can barely contain the excitement.

Your aim should be to discover what makes you excited and begin to perfect it. Determine your talent in life and prepare to master it. And always see to improve your natural abilities to perfect them—focus on your strengths, not your weaknesses. The world's best athletes. They train to become better at what they're naturally good at—and what they enjoy doing—every single day. They stick to what they do best and gain rewards because of it.

There are only two phases to a life of fulfillment: determine your talent and perfect it. Doing those two things will pave the way to your receiving the satisfaction and contentment you were meant to have. "A man's true delight is to do the things he was made for."[118]

Create a Personal Growth Plan for Success

Having a goal begins with knowing what you want out of life, but it takes more than having a goal to achieve that goal. There are plenty of people who know what they want but still aren't successful. You need a personal growth plan to help you reach your maximum potential and fulfill God's plan for your life. It's not only knowing what you should do, but also, it's about

[118] https://quotefancy.com/quote/859554/Marcus-Aurelius-A-man-s-true-delight-is-to-do-the-things-he-was-made-for

growing in that area to make the best use of and highlight the things you do well. That's continual personal growth.

Personal growth is not an automatic process. If growth is going to happen, it needs to be intentional. Having a personal development plan will change your life. The only way you will continue to learn and grow is to commit to it. Highly successful people have a constant longing for information and are always asking questions and seeking solutions. Successful people set goals with timelines, wake up early each morning, and take action steps.

What is done today determines success for tomorrow and years to come. Success isn't a secret or something for a select few. It's both possible and attainable for everybody, but it starts with this declaration: the secret of success is determined by a daily routine, by what is done—today.

I believe this important principle connects so much to your purpose that I wrote a book about it entitled *Pursing Your Purpose*, and in the book, I write about how important it is to live a life of purpose.

Every day people are either restoring or preparing. Every day people are either trying to fix yesterday—relationships, issues, priorities, lost opportunities—or they are living their life in such a way that they are preparing for tomorrow and setting up a routine to ensure daily success is practically a given.

Highly successful people know what they want out of life. Not only do they grow to their full potential, but they also plant seeds that help others. They don't live only for themselves. They're a waterway, not a reservoir. They know what significance is, and significance is adding value to other people's lives.

The road to becoming your best, most successful self can feel challenging at times, and it can take a lot out of you. You will encounter periods of weariness and discouragement and wanting to give up. However, it is important to believe success is possible because as you continue your journey, you will eventually embark upon those moments. Having a personal development plan in place will help you stay on track to living a life of power, purpose, and victory.

To progress in your personal growth, you must consider who you are spending your time with on a regular basis. Here's a bit of wisdom from the book of Proverbs, "Walk with the wise and become wise, for a companion of fools suffers harm,"[119] and a bit of advice from business philosopher Jim Rohn, "You are the average of the five people you spend the most time with."[120]

Who are you spending your time with? This is where you have to take your time and carefully consider your responses to this question and write down your answer. Please don't take your personal growth lightly; it takes boldness, courage, and sacrifice to embark upon this journey of becoming your best self. When you develop the fearlessness and strength to do it, you will gain confidence. Start writing those names now. For the sake of following Rohn's advice, list the five people you spend the most time with:

1.

---

[119] Proverbs 13:20, NIV

[120] http://www.psychology24.org/are-you-really-the-average-of-the-five-people-you-spend-most-time-with/

2.

3.

4.

5.

Practicing Positive Thinking

Positive thinking is a mental attitude in which you expect good and favorable results. In other words, positive thinking is the process of forming thoughts that create and transform positive energy into reality. A positive mind expects happiness, good health, and a happy ending in any situation.

Positive thinking forces the mind to ignore the negative and focus on things that are productive, things that will give you positive results. According to some medical experts, thinking positively will add to your happiness, your health, and your success. Consider these health benefits of positive thinking as reported by Mayo Clinic:[121]

- Increased life span
- Lower rates of depression
- Lower levels of distress

---

[121] http://www.mayoclinic.org/healthy-lifestyle/stress-management/in-depth/positive-thinking/art-20043950

- Greater resistance to the common cold
- Better psychological and physical well-being
- Better cardiovascular health and reduced risk of death from cardiovascular disease
- Better coping skills during hardships and times of stress

Positive thinking gives you confidence and boldness. You can always tell someone who is a positive thinker just by the way you walk and talk. They hold their heads high, they have great posture, and their voice has power when they speak. Overall, their body language reveals a positive attitude. More and more you find that motivational speakers and leadership conferences are stressing the importance of being around positive-thinking people. Here's some advice to help you succeed with positive thinking.

Do your homework. Get as much information as possible about the power of positive thinking, and consider all you will gain from applying it to your thinking process. Then convince yourself to do it. It is a force that will change your life. Even if you are not sure about the idea, still go for it. You have nothing to lose.

Do it for you. Don't worry about what other people might say or think about you when they notice the change in your thinking. Some people may not understand or approve, but don't allow that to deter you. Just keep going forward.

Train your mind to see only things that will benefit you. If you have to put an imaginary barrier on both sides to do this, go ahead. To succeed at thinking for positive outcomes all the time, you need to have single-minded vision.

Speak positively. Self-talk is the key to developing positive thinking. It also helps when you only use positive words in your conversation with others. Don't waste time on idle conversation, especially if others are not on the same page.

Smile. And do it as often as possible, because this will help you to stay on a path of positive thinking. And it will show how kind and approachable you are.

It takes work to master positive thinking. It won't happen overnight. If a negative thought happens to penetrate your thinking, try to reverse it with a positive one. If it returns, change it again. Treat it as though there are two images in front of you, and you have to make a choice. If you persevere, eventually you'll only see one image in front of you—and it will be a positive one.

If it gets too hard, if something occurs that prevents you from changing your disposition and outlook from negative to positive, do not give up. Keep looking only to all the profit you will ultimately gain from it. It doesn't matter what your current situation happens to be. Keep thinking positively. Have an expectation that things will change for the good, and what you're looking for will happen in due time. If you continue on that path, you will modify the way your mind thinks. It might take a little while to see the change, but eventually it will happen.

When people look at you, they should see a winner, someone who is going to be successful. Positive thinking will help people see you as you are. Positive thinking will also give you hope, clarity, optimism, and passion—everything you need to become the winner you are.

Chapter Twelve: Act Like You Won

"If you don't see yourself as a winner, then you cannot perform as a winner."

~Zig Ziglar

Remember, it's not just how you see yourself that counts in your quest to become a winner, but it's also how others see you. I talked about the importance of first impressions a few chapters ago. I want to pick up on that notion here. Now, this may sound shallow to your ears, but, believe it or not, how you dress says a lot about you. It's an important part of making a first great impression and leaving a lasting one. It's nothing new, and certainly nothing I made up. It's just a way life. And the careers editor for *Business Insider* even wrote about it.

> "Research shows that your appearance strongly influences other people's perception of your financial success, authority, trustworthiness, intelligence, and suitability for hire or promotion. And, because perception is often reality, what you wear not only communicates who are you are in the minds of others, but also influences your level of career advancement. Research also found that when you combine your appearance with communication skills, not only is

> others' perception of you affected, but their behavior toward you is also influence."[122]

You see, I'm not making it up.

While our clothing doesn't determine our value as individuals, in a world that often judges a book by its cover, how we dress does matter. And it matters a lot. That's why it's one of the things I want to talk about in this chapter. It's a relatively easy way to begin to carry yourself as though you've already won. I'd like to share some other challenging things you must do to ensure the victory that's essentially yours. So, let's get started.

Dress Like You Won

You may not think people are looking at you, but let me tell you someone is *always* looking at you. People tend to size you up based on how you dress and carry yourself. The person is either fascinated or thinks you could use a little help.

I've concluded, after watching many movies and television shows, that you never know who's genuine and who is not. For instance, if you observe people in public settings and try to determine who is genuine in their character and/or presentation, you may find that those whom you believe to be genuine are not and vice versa. The point I'm trying to make is that it does not matter if you have it all together or not. If you learn how to dress and look like you've got it all together, opportunities will come knocking at your door. You don't have to go out and purchase expensive clothing to do it, and

---

[122] BusinessInsider.com, "Here's How Your Clothing Affects Your Success," Jacquelyn Smith, Aug. 19, 2014, 10:52 a.m.

you don't have to dress like a supermodel or movie star. However, you do need to "dress to impress" if you want to excel in certain areas.

I realize that some people are good at putting together an outfit and selecting the right accessories that will help them appear classy and sophisticated, while others are not. If you don't fall into the former category, take some time and learn how to dress in a sophisticated or business-like fashion. We are all actors in one way or another, so learn to dress as if you've won already. Ask a friend or relative whom you believe often presents themselves well to help you if you don't know where to begin. Trust me, that person will be happy to do so.

One of the first things you must do to ensure you always have a polished look is to make sure your clothes fit. Now, most clothes you buy off the rack are not going to fit—particularly if they're not high-priced designer clothing. The pant legs might be too long, or there's too much room under your arms. Tailoring is the quick and easy way to solve that problem. Your local dry cleaner usually offers that service. If that's not in your budget, you can also research and shop at clothing stores that offer tailoring as a free service when you make a purchase. If you still think that's too much, the following are a few tips from WikiHow.com I found, for ensuring you buy clothes that fit your body.

Know your body measurements. Find a tailor, seamstress or a friend with a measuring tape to help you to determine your measurements (i.e. chest, waist, arm length, inseam, collar, etc.). Second, don't fully rely on the sizes on the tags. Did you know that sizes vary according to the designer and that some designers even fudge the number to appeal to our vanity? That's right, if you're rejoicing because you could get into a size eight recently, it just might be a size ten or twelve you're wearing. I want to stress here, that the size doesn't matter. What is important is that it fits and that you look good in it. Remember, you are dressing as if you've already won, so make it count whether you're a size four or a size fourteen, whether your waistline is a 32 or a 42.

Third, read the store's sizing charts if it has one. You can then compare their charts against your measurements to determine what size item you should try on. Fourth, if you just cannot find that perfect size off the rack, buy clothing for your biggest part; then take them to a tailor (if you can) to have them fixed for a perfect fit. Fifth, it goes without saying that you should always try on something before you buy it. There's nothing worse than buying something you think fits, only to get home and discover it looks awful on you and then have to take it back. Sixth, get a second opinion. Take someone shopping with you, or ask another shopper in the store (if you ask the salesperson, he or she just might tell you anything to get the sale). Seven, buy custom clothing online. Find retailers you can submit your measurements to and get clothing truly made just for your body.[123] People admire you when you wear an outfit that looks as though it were made for you. So much so, that you could get almost whatever you want just by the way you dress.

I believe a well-dressed person is an impressive sight. It's no comparison to someone who doesn't care about his or her appearance. The bottom line is how you look speaks volumes about how you think about yourself. When someone is evaluating you, I believe at least forty percent or so form opinions based on outward appearance and how you carry

---

[123] Wikihow.com, "shopping for the right clothing"

yourself. Make no mistake: if you dress as if you've won, you will be a winner.

Walk Like You Won

I never thought the way you walk could make a difference in whether you succeed or not until I did the research and adjusted my walk to test that theory. Your walk, just like your dress, says a lot about you. If you stroll with slumped shoulders and your head down all the time, you can convey to others that you're insecure or don't want to be bothered. If you walk fast and always seem to be in a rush, you may convey that you're anxious and overwhelmed—that you need to relax. If you walk with your head up, shoulders squared, generally making eye contact with people as you pass them by, you exude confidence and trustworthiness; you're signaling that you're approachable.

After adjusting my walking posture, I witnessed the tremendous difference in others' reactions toward me. If you examine your walk and make a few positive changes (that is, if you find that you need to), not only will it send a signal to others that you are a winner, but it will also go a long way in making you feel good about yourself and where you're headed. Here are a couple of suggestions for improving the manner of your gait.

- When you are walking, stand straight and upright like you are proud. Keep your shoulders pulled back but relaxed. Swing your arms comfortably as you walk. Look confident *but don't act conceited*, as people are taking mental notes of you as you walk.

- Walk like you're in the military. That is something I know firsthand because I spent time in the military. The military masters excellence in everything they do. And one of the ways that excellence is demonstrated is in the posture and walk of a soldier. Have you ever noticed how succinct their movements are, and how coordinated they are when they walk together? They maintain that strict composure in virtually all situations. They salute each other upon encounter. I've always found that to be fascinating and encouraging, and the principle of excellence that drives that attitude isn't just for military personnel. People admire the discipline and control of keeping your composure. You can tell the difference between a soldier and a citizen just by the walk. Soldiers walk like they are somebody. And so can you.

Talk Like You Won

Can you recall your first encounter with someone, when you were either impressed or turned off by the first thing they said to you? First impressions include first expressions, and like the former, our initial words can determine the direction we go, whether it's after a job interview or in a new friendship. People tend always to remember their first conversation with you.

If you want to be a winner, talk like one. Speak confidently, be concise, and try not to repeat yourself. Give the appearance that you truly know what you are saying right from the beginning, even if you may not know all of what you are saying. Of course, knowing all about what you're saying can be helpful, but to appear confident in what you are saying matters more. And the key here is to talk about what you know. If you are not sure about a certain topic, one of the worse things you can do is pretend to, especially with someone who is very knowledgeable about it. You will only come off looking ignorant, and that is not the lasting impression you want to leave with others. If you get nervous before you have to engage in a conversation with someone you're meeting for the first time, or you struggle with small talk, try doing this: go over what you want to say in your mind until you feel comfortable with the conversation you are about to participate in. Planning what you're going to say also helps to avoid an awkward conversation with someone. It helps to ensure you say the right words, because once you start speaking, you can't take back your words. The most successful motivational and inspirational speakers look great on stage because they spend an enormous amount of time preparing; repeatedly they go over what they will say, so why shouldn't you? Singer Brian McKnight said, "I was brought up to be a gentleman. That means you know how to walk, talk and dress the part."

I remember once being challenged by a close friend about my thinking and speaking as if I had already obtained all that I could imagine. My friend didn't understand the concept of speaking things into existence. You should never feel afraid to present yourself confidently with what you want and believe. Oprah Winfrey said, "You don't get in life what you want, you get what you believe." And I agree with her.

A study published in the *Journal of Organizational Behavior and Human Decision Processes* found that people will believe in a noticeably confident speaker before they will believe someone who's more knowledgeable.

When I watch a political debate, I often think the candidates have no idea what they are talking about, but they speak with authority to come across as trustworthy. If they just state the facts, they might seem too defensive if they aren't presented the right way. Sure, you should use facts if you have them, but keep your confidence in the forefront. The more you look confident in what you're talking about, the higher your chances you'll come out a winner.

Hang with Winners

It has been said that if you want to know a person, look at the people they hang out with. You've likely heard one of these sayings: "Birds of a feather flock together," Sheep school together," or "pigs trample a lot of dirt together."

More often than not, people who like what they do keep a smile on their faces. They never complain that life has dealt them a bad hand. These are the same individuals who are content with where they are in life. They are winners. They don't have to act phony; it's how they are. And winners seem to hang out in the same places. If you find one, you will find another.

If you are consistently surrounded by negative people, you won't have a winning attitude for long. Even if you start out with one, you'll soon find that you're thinking and acting like the people you're around. But it's more likely that a winner won't stick around negative folks. They quickly find their own. It's highly unlikely that you'll see a negative thinking person in the company of winners. It would be like trying to mix oil and water—they don't. Groups like country clubs and lodges seem to attract like-minded people with a winning mindset.

Most successful groups have one thing in common: their primary goal is to succeed. You know the old saying "one bad apple spoils the whole bunch". Well, if you want to make a positive change, you need to get rid of the negative one and concentrate on the positive one.

When you have a winning attitude, you tend to attract like-minded people into your circle. They notice something positive in you, and as a result, they want to connect. The same goes for people who have a pessimistic outlook. If you always have a sour look on your face and complain a lot, you will likely attract similar people to you.

Chapter Thirteen: No Pain, No Gain

"Pain is Temporary, Quitting Lasts Forever"

~Lance Armstrong

If it's worth it to you to be a winner in life, you must know it will be a struggle. The cost will be great, and the pain will be high. To overcome any struggle and live a victorious life will not be a walk in the park, but if you're up for the challenge, I promise you it that will be worth it.

Imagine you're inside a furniture store where you're taken in by the beauty and freshness of all the beautiful pieces in the showroom—a leather chesterfield sofa, glass coffee tables, a traditional bedroom set that appears to be made of solid oak. Now stop right there and focus on the phrase "appears to be." If you know anything about furniture, you know that you can have two pieces of furniture that look equally beautiful but not be equal in quality or value. Depending on what kind of furniture store you walk into, you can be misled by great lighting and professional arrangement. You might believe what you're looking at in the showroom is top quality. However, if you're not careful and don't know what you are looking for exactly, you will end up purchasing lesser quality furniture at boutique shop prices, thinking you are getting a good deal when in reality you got tricked by appearance.

One way of determining the quality of something is noting how long it will last with almost the same look and function as when it was purchased. Most things break down with time; however, high-quality products last a long time—and look good for a long time. When they get old, they become antiques, which typically increase in value. But keep in mind that there is a price to pay for quality.

Becoming a winner will cost you a great deal, but it will be a permanent win if you do it the correct way.

Winners never settle or compromise when it comes to meeting their ultimate goal. They realize that compromising will only cost them more in the long run. It might take a longer time than the norm. It just might be a bit harder than what you are accustomed to. But winners know how to pursue their purpose no matter the obstacles before them. They remain focused on the bigger picture.

Here are some specific things that winners do.

Let go of the past. Winners don't replay memories of their past mistakes. They realize space is needed for more productive thinking to accomplish their goals. Keeping a record of the bad things that occurred in your past will only prevent you from being a true winner in life. I realize that some things are hard to forget, however it's necessary to leave your past right where it is—behind you—and concentrate on the future. You can't move forward and backward at the same time, and still expect to live like a winner. It's like burning the candle on both ends. Now that you realize this, write down some of the past things you may have been holding on to and need to let go of.

____

____

____

Think Positively. Winners stay positive. Thinking negatively and worrying only hurts you; it does not improve your odds of moving into the winners' circle. Constant feelings of discontent, discouragement, sadness, anger, and so on will prevent you from being successful in most areas of your lives, from professional, to personal, to spiritual. Are you bombarded by negative thoughts? Write down any negative thoughts you know you need to change.

Make good decisions. Learn how to solve and settle future problems as quickly as possible and then move forward, toward your destiny. Do it quickly and precisely. If it's not profiting you by keeping the memory of it, forget about it and keep moving. Your destiny is waiting. Write down some of the areas in which you need to make better decisions.

Make a commitment. Winners are committed to the process of being successful. Assess your weaknesses and your strengths—and be honest with yourself. Then commit today to do whatever it takes to get closer to fulfilling an abandoned dream. Your success or your failure depends on your commitment. Develop a realistic plan, set some markers for measuring your progress, and be in it for the long haul. Commit to winning. Write down some of the things you're willing to commit to doing to reach your destiny.

Take Responsibility. Winners are disciplined. They prioritize their time and rarely waste it on frivolous activities. How you spend your time is important. Surfing social media, shopping, talking on the phone, texting and hanging out with friends aren't bad things—but they have their place and time. If you are serious about achieving your goals, those things should not consume most of your day. You must take complete responsibility for how you spend your time. Remember, you cannot get back yesterday and tomorrow is not promised. Once you take responsibility for your time and your actions, and become serious about meeting your goal, you will see the bigger picture and begin to make the sacrifices necessary for fulfilling your goals. In the space below, write down some of the things you believe you are spending too much time on and are willing to take responsibility for and change.

After you finish examining where you are and adjusting habits to position yourself for success, decide you won't ever let someone else be the one to say "when" for you. Others can be helpful, but only you know when it's time to say when. You hold the key to your success. If you truly desire to change yourself and your life, then start with your mind. Whatever the mind does, the body will follow.

Remember this: failure is not the worst thing that can happen to you, not trying and wasting your entire life is. When you decide to take control your life instead of just settling and barely surviving, you will experience the beauty of discovering how wonderful life can be.

Get Comfortable

The search for success and happiness can be challenging and overwhelming, yet we are striving to get there. We are willing to go through the necessary transitions to gain peace of mind, the kind of peace that transcends our understanding where there is no anger, no fear, and no guilt. We want to go to sleep at night and rest comfortably, so that when we wake up in the morning, there's no worry about how we're going to pay our next bill.

I've heard so many people say, "I need a vacation" but can't afford it, or "I went on a vacation, but when I returned, I almost felt like I made a mistake because I'm up to my neck in bills."

What I want you to understand is that we have to work early and play later, work hard and then enjoy. If you haven't put in the work, it will be difficult to truly afford and enjoy a vacation, a luxurious one at that. And you must put in the work in all areas of your life.

Success is nothing without good health and the ability to enjoy what you have acquired. It makes no sense to endure the pain going through the process, but when it's time to reap what you've sown, your health is preventing you from enjoying it. According to P.T Barnum, "the foundation of success in life is good health: that is the substratum fortune, it is also the basis of happiness. A person cannot accumulate a fortune very well when he is sick." So, I say this to you, eat right, exercise, and live a healthy life. I want to see you enjoy life after you have put in the work.

Becoming Financially Free

I've talked quite a bit about the obstacles of self-doubt, procrastination, and fear, but another significant barrier to winning can be our finances. I realize this book is not about managing your finances, but I want to say a few things about the importance of gaining financial freedom on the road to success in your life.

Financial freedom is the ability to maintain the lifestyle you desire in the absence of a regular paycheck. It allows you to make major life decisions without worrying about money.

According to the Bible, money answers all things. And when you look at it, it certainly does. But here is the kicker, you need to have enough money to answer all things without wondering where you are going to get more money to do what you want to do. Let's face it: it's nice to have enough money to go on a vacation whenever and wherever you want to, to shop and buy whatever you desire. But for that to become a reality in your life, you may need to re-program what was instilled into your thinking from a young age about managing money, particularly if you haven't been the best at managing it.

If you are like most of us, you were likely told by your parents from a young age to get an education and then find a job. You did what they said, hoping that after all that knowledge you gained from school, you would land a good job, save a little from each paycheck for about forty or so years until to you reached sixty-five, then retire hoping you would have enough to live comfortably for the rest of your life.

That path probably would look more like this: you spend most of your day every day working for some company, trying to move up the ladder, begging the boss for a raise, and praying you have enough to buy a house. And after all that, you fill the house with unnecessary stuff. Only then do you realize that there has been no exploring, little relaxing, or spending enough quality time with family—and you're not retiring financially free.

I can't speak for you or anyone else, but I know the traditional path to retirement won't work for me. And I hope after taking a realistic picture of what that looks like, you'll decide it won't work for you either. Instead of accumulating material things that will eventually fade away, I prefer freedom—financial freedom. Yes, it is the way to go. Here's what that looks like: having the freedom to start a business if you desire, take some time off just because you want to, or travel the world. It's not about what you choose to do as much as it's about having the freedom to choose and do whatever you want whenever you want.

As I stated earlier, financial bondage can be counted among the things that can keep us from fulfilling our goals. For example, if one of your goals is to stop renting and purchase a house. If you have more debt than income or a low credit score due to not paying your bills on time, you likely will not qualify for a mortgage loan.

If your finances are holding you back from achieving your goals, please check out the books and money management ministries of Mary Hunt, Dave Ramsey, or Crown Ministries. They all provide great resources that can help you begin to think differently about money (which is the key to gaining financial freedom) and do what's necessary to get debt free once and for all.

A New Beginning

I have a few last words to share, but this is certainly not the end.

Today is the start of a new chapter in your life. Yes, I know you've reached the end of this book, but if you're serious about changing your thinking to change your outcome for a promised future (and you've got to be if you're still with me), you are just at the beginning. The value of any book, conference, or seminar you invest in is the impact it has on your life.

Could it be that the reason you decided to dive into this book is that you desperately want a change in your thinking? Maybe you want to improve some area your life. Or maybe you want to move from experiencing mediocre outcomes to experiencing exceptional outcomes in your career or business. Whatever the reason, it's now time to do the work.

Let's face it: there's no miracle that you will accrue just by reading any book. You must practice and apply what you've read and learned for any of this to work in your favor. I can promise you this: if you work at it and allow God to guide you through the process, within no time you will see progress and enjoy a level of success that will exceed your expectations.

We discussed winning, desires, dreams, attitude, and gratitude. We also talked about living life and the mind games the enemy will throw at you to detour you from your destiny. I've shown you how to make good decisions and how important your thinking is to get the results you desire. You read about how positive thinking can make an impact in your life. You even now know the importance of dressing like a winner, walking like a winner and talking like a winner even if that's not how you always feel. In other words, you now know that you can "act" your way into success until your hopes, dreams, and reality all line up.

If you need to re-read this book or revisit certain sections, I encourage you to do so. I'm sure some concepts may jump out at you the second time around that you may have overlooked the first time you read the book. Most of all, I want you to begin practicing what you've learned. The words I've shared mean very little if you don't apply them.

I want to leave you with these two quotes:

"There are two types of people who will tell you that you cannot make a difference in this world: those who are afraid to try and those who are afraid you will succeed."

~Ray Goforth

"Don't be afraid to give up the good to go for the great."

John D. Rockefeller

May the success you gain from this book surpass all that you can ever imagine. Blessings upon you!

89601662R00126

Made in the USA
Columbia, SC
22 February 2018